The People Called Baptists

BY

GEO. W. McDANIEL

Author of "Our Boys in France"

2412

THE SUNDAY SCHOOL BOARD
OF THE
SOUTHERN BAPTIST CONVENTION
NASHVILLE, TENN.

TO

MARY SCARBOROUGH McDANIEL

THE

DEAREST OF DAUGHTERS

Foreword

This book contains a vigorous statement of the principles and history of the People Called Baptists. It also rings clear and loud with a call to these same people to vindicate their glorious doctrines by equally glorious deeds. The author is well and widely known for his strong grip on any subject he handles, and for an awakening and captivating style. These qualities are pregnant throughout the pages of this book. The author has a message. He knows well what it is. He believes it is worth delivering, and he does it in an earnest, forthwith way. He is not ornate. He is too earnest to be.

There is a fine tonic in the pages of this book for the sleepy, come-easy, go-easy souls, desiring above all things to prevent anything out of the dull ordinary from happening.

The Baptist people are vindicated in their origin, history and achievements. Their principles are set out with admirable frankness, clearness and in excellent temper.

The author sets the Baptists right on the Union question, on their loyalty to government, and gives them high praise for their age-long devotion to the principle of full and equal religious liberty to all.

His treatment of the aggression of the government on the liberties of Baptists and others during the war just ending is timely and very forceful. Things have gone far wrong at Washington along religious lines, and this volume discusses very vigorously the principles involved. Dr. McDaniel makes the matter plain. He calls the government down, as we all must do.

The whole assembly of discussions is calculated to inform and stimulate the Baptist people, and will make excellent reading for other peoples, multitudes of whom dreadfully need to know what is so lucidly stated in this volume. "The People Called Baptists" is a present-day book. It covers present truths, especially needed now when so many are trying to obscure the truth by enveloping the whole land in a dense fog of sentimentalism. Dr. McDaniel is pastor of the great old First Baptist Church, Richmond, Virginia, than which there is perhaps not a greater church in the land, and he in this book invites the public to sit down at the same table with his home-folks and eat out of the same dishes. My hope is there will be a full table, for the food prepared is calculated to make all who partake of it strong. There is much good meat here for people of sound digestion.

J. B. GAMBRELL.

Southwestern Baptist Theological Seminary, Fort Worth, Texas.

Introduction

Horace Greeley, commenting upon Solomon's "Of making many books there is no end," once remarked "Though there is happily a speedy end of most books after they are made." Publishers can verify Mr. Greeley's statement. Why, then, venture this book?

The eagerness with which my own congregation sought for copies of doctrinal discussions; the proposal of a far-seeing layman that a book be written on the position of Baptists in the present crisis; the application by many for the presentation, in tract form, of an address delivered before the Baptist Council of Richmond; the misunderstanding of Baptist tenets by Christians of other denominations; and a renewed conviction of our duty to teach and to train our growing constituency; these facts, briefly stated, explain the appearance of this volume.

In other decades Baptists were better indoctrinated than they are to-day. The environment in which they lived, sometimes inimicable to them, was conducive to the mastery of their principles. Of later years, a tendency to depreciate doctrinal discussion is easily discernible, and young converts particularly are not rooted and grounded in the faith. Modern nonchalance acts as if it made little difference what one believes. With cavalier air it belittles the man who has the temerity to make a denominational affirmation. The opinion of the author is that character

and destiny are determined by what one believes and
that a faith not worth fighting for is not worth having.
Herein are adduced the considerations that make
Baptists a peculiar people; herein are narrated some
of their achievements; and herein is discussed their
proper attitude towards the issues of the day. To
detail my indebtedness for these contents is useless
and impossible. Former teachers, cherished friends,
and various books have been very helpful. Probably
there are sources to which I am unconsciously under
obligation. If this book is of God, it will live; if it
is not, I should want it to die.

The People Called Baptists

The People Called Baptists

I.

WHO THEY ARE: WHAT THEY HAVE DONE.

The name "Christians" was first applied, in derision, to the followers of Christ, by enemies at Antioch. The name "Baptists" was first given, in ridicule, by Pedo-baptist opponents of the people who rejected the baptism of babes. Both names, like the cross, have been changed from marks of shame to badges of honor.

The distinguishing principles of the people first called "Christians" and now called "Baptists" are:

1. The Scriptures, the only authoritative guide-book for our religious life. There may be no appeal from, or addition to, their precepts and principles.

2. The individual and direct access of every soul to God; none between man and God, save only the God-man.

3. The complete separation of Church and State in their respective fields; the Church

dealing with religious, the State with civil affairs.

4. The simple polity of the church's government; each church autonomous and a democracy in itself.

5. The baptism of believers only, or a regenerate church membership. Incidentally, they believe in baptism by immersion only, according to the Scriptures, as symbolizing the death, burial and resurrection of Christ; and that the Lord's Supper is a church ordinance.

A Noble Ancestry.

To be well born is to enter life with advantage. Baptists are justly proud of their parentage—the New Testament. They have an ancient and scriptural origin. Certain characters in history are named as founders of various denominations: The Disciples began with Alexander Campbell, the Methodists with John Wesley, the Presbyterians with John Calvin, the Lutherans with Martin Luther, and the Church of England with Henry VIII and Cranmer's Book of Common Prayer in the reign of Edward VI. Not so

with the Baptists. There is no personality
this side of Jesus Christ who is a satisfactory
explanation of their origin. The New Testament churches were independent, self-governing, democratic bodies like the Baptist
churches of to-day. We originated, not at
the Reformation, nor in the Dark Ages, nor
in any century after the Apostles, but our
marching orders are the Commission, and the
first Baptist church was the church at Jerusalem. Our principles are as old as Christianity, and we acknowledge no founder
but Christ.

An Honorable History.

Character is determined by ideals and
achievements. If we would know the place
of Baptists, we must consider their historic
greatness, their heroic fidelity to human
liberty and their part in the life of the world.
Our principles develop a type of character
and life which tends to make men potent
factors in achievements worth while.

Baptists have been pioneers in so many
fields that to enumerate these might seem to

assume a braggart spirit. But a statement
of irrefutable facts must be taken as dis-
passionate and impartial. Baptists have always been champions of civil and religious
liberty. Roger Williams, who took ground
in advance of his Puritan compeers on the
subject of personal liberty, being banished
from the colony of Massachusetts, went to
the present site of Providence, Rhode Island,
where he founded what is regarded by some
as the first Baptist Church in America, and
the first commonwealth on earth in which
there was absolute civil and religious liberty.
The framers of the Constitution of the United
States caught the spirit of Roger Williams
and as a result we have a country which has
been the refuge of the persecuted and oppressed of all nations. Article VI. on religious liberty in the American Constitution
was introduced into it by the united effort
of Baptists in 1789. The first amendment to
the Constitution of the United States, guar-
anteeing freedom of speech, freedom of religion, and the right to petition, was adopted
largely through the activity of Baptists.
They took the initiative in a letter to President

Washington and a month later Madison, with Washington's approval, presented the amendment.

John Clarke, highly educated in arts and in medicine, the most outright and upright, important and influential American Baptist of the seventeenth century, did more than anyone else to call the attention of the world to Puritan intolerance. He secured the Charter of 1643 which made Rhode Island a free democratic State with full provision for liberty of conscience, and he was the originator of the public free school system. He founded the Newport church, which, for consistent and persistent devotion to Baptist principles, for completeness of organization and fervor in evangelism, deserves the priority.

The father of modern missions was William Carey, an English Baptist. In thirty years he and his co-laborers made the Word of God accessible to a third of the people of the globe. He was "one of England's greatest men, doing more to make the India of to-day than Clive or Hastings, and contributing to the making of England hardly less than John Wesley."

Organic foreign missions in America began with the "American Board of Commissioners for Foreign Missions" (1810). Two of these were Adoniram Judson and Luther Rice. Judson and his wife, studying their Greek New Testament, became convinced that the immersion of a professing believer is the only Christian baptism. They were baptized by a Baptist missionary in India. Rice, upon reaching his destination, arrived at a similar conclusion. Luther Rice is noted as a missionary and the founder of the old Columbian College, Washington, D. C., and Adoniram Judson is the foremost name in the annals of American missions.

The first president of Harvard College was Henry Dunster, who, by his enthusiasm and by sacrificing his means and health for its interest, brought the college into a position exceeding the hopes of its best friends. He lost his office because of his espousal of Baptist views. The largest early benefactors of Harvard College were Thomas Hollis, a wealthy English Baptist, and his descendants.

He founded the Hollis Chair of Theology, the first in the United States.

The man who snatched the Southwest from Mexico and handed back to the United States what is now Texas, part of New Mexico, Oklahoma, Kansas, Colorado and Wyoming was General Sam Houston, a loyal Baptist. Nathaniel Macon, pronounced by John Randolph and John Jay among the very wisest of men they had known and whom Randolph in his last days called the best and purest man he had ever met, was a Baptist.

President Abraham Lincoln attributed all that he was to a Baptist mother. President Jefferson Davis devoted the ground where he was born in Kentucky as the site for a Baptist Church and it is so used now. At the dedication of the building he delivered an address and stated that perhaps some people wondered why he, who was not a Baptist, should be so interested in that faith. He explained thus: "My father, who was a better man than I am, was a Baptist." Henry Clay, President Arthur and Justice Hughes were the sons of Baptist preachers. William Jennings Bryan's and William Howard Taft's fathers were Baptists. General Madison, brother of President Madison, was a Baptist; so was Mrs. Woodson, the favorite aunt of Jefferson. Thomas, when young, loved to visit her house in Goochland County and to attend the Baptist Church with her. Major General Tasker Bliss, one of the American peace commissioners at Versailles, is the son of a former professor in Rochester Theological Seminary. Major General William Graves, head of the American forces in Russia, is a Baptist and a graduate of Baylor University. Lloyd-George, who piloted the British ship of State through the stormy seas of the world's worst war, says of himself: "I am a Baptist."

Bible societies were originated first by a Baptist, Joseph Hughes. The International Uniform Sunday School Lesson System is due to a Baptist layman of Chicago, B. F. Jacobs. The first Sunday School paper for young people in the United States, "The Young Reaper," was established by Baptists. The Baraca movement was started by a Baptist layman, Marshal A. Hudson.

Sir Henry Havelock, the valiant British general and the deliverer of Lucknow, united with the Baptists of India and was baptized by one of Carey's fellow missionaries. In Cromwell's Irish garrisons there were twelve Baptist governors of cities, ten colonels, three lieutenant-colonels, ten majors, and forty-three company officers. In the War of the Commonwealth in England and the War of the Revolution in the United States, Baptists were all patriots.

Among the many Baptists who rendered military service in the Revolution, a few conspicuous names may be mentioned. Pastor M'Clanahan, of Culpeper County, Virginia, raised a military company of Baptists and served on the field, both as captain and chaplain. Reverend David Barrow shouldered his musket and showed how fields were won. Colonel Jacob Houghton, grandfather of Spencer Cone, was in a Baptist meeting-house when the news of the defeat of Lexington reached him. The services ended, he stood in the open before the building and spoke: "Men of New Jersey, the Red Coats are murdering our brethren in New England. Who follows me to Boston?" Every man stepped into line and answered, "I." General

Scriven, when ordered by the British officer to give up Sunbury, near Savannah, sent back the answer, "Come and take it." Deacon Mills, of the First Baptist Church of Philadelphia, commanded skilfully one thousand riflemen at the battle of Long Island and for his valor was made a brigadier general. Deacon Loxley, of the same church, commanded the artillery at the battle of Germantown with the rank of colonel. "He was always foremost when great guns were in question." Add to this galaxy John Hart, who signed the Declaration of Independence, and John Brown, whose fleet of privately owned vessels attacked the Gaspee which had entered Narragansett Bay to enforce British revenue customs. Lieutenant Duddington was wounded, the other officers and the crew left and the Gaspee was blown up. "This was the first British blood shed in the War of Independence." In their list of Tory sympathizers made up by Judge Curwen appear nine hundred and twenty-six names living in America, and a larger number were already exiled by Colonial law, but there is not the name of one Baptist on the list. This is why

President Washington, in his letter to the Baptists, could pay them the just tribute: "I recollect with satisfaction that the religious societies of which you are a member have been, throughout America, uniformly and almost unanimously, the firm friends to civil liberty, and the persevering promoters of our glorious Revolution." It explains how Thomas Jefferson could write to a Baptist Church, "We have acted *together* from the origin to the end of a memorable Revolution."

Baptists are renowned the world over for their loyalty. At the coronation of the late Czar at Moscow, May 15, 1895, fear filled all hearts, and it was not known who was loyal. Someone told a prominent officer that he could trust the Baptists. Many of them were therefore chosen, some of whom had just returned from exile and were drafted for this special service. William of Orange was sustained in the gloomiest hours of his struggles for the Dutch Republic by the sympathy and aid of the Baptists. He testified to their loyalty, industry and virtue.

Baptist loyalty to country has met the test in the present war. State and General Con-

ventions, without exception, have rung true
in patriotic resolutions. Our churches have
backed the war with their money and their
members. Pacifist pastors were few and without weight in the councils of the denomination
or churches. Hundreds of ministers have
served in various capacities, some as military
combatants. Patriotic fervor burned in the
Theological Seminaries and their students
enlisted in large proportions. Our sons went
to war by the ten thousands, and they went
with the benediction of the denomination
upon their heads. Our daughters donned and
adorned the Red Cross and alleviated human
suffering. The soil of France is enriched with
Baptist blood. America's name is made
more glorious by Baptist devotion. And all
of this was done in spite of certain governmental acts which we could not and did not
approve.

The Christian pulpit has been occupied by
able and eloquent Baptists. Alexander Mc-
Laren, famous as the greatest biblical ser-
monizer of a century; F. B. Meyer, whose
preaching and writing have circled the globe;
A. J. Gordon, who has been called a titanic

expounder of God's Word; Andrew Fuller, who held the rope while Carey went down in the well; Robert Hall, whose elegant diction is unsurpassed by any English orator; Christmas Evans, whose impassioned eloquence won thousands to Christ; and Charles Spurgeon, whose sermons were heard and read by more people than those of any other preacher of all time, were all Baptist preachers. Dr. Chalmers said of the English Baptist preachers of his day: "Perhaps there is not a more intellectual community of ministers in our island, or who have put forth to their number a greater amount of mental power and mental activity in the defense and illustration of our common faith."

The largest contribution of the New World to civilization was the principle of separation of Church and State. Historians ascribe to the Baptists the chief credit for the establishment of this principle in the United States. John Locke said: "The Baptists were the first propounders of an absolute liberty, just and true liberty, equal and impartial liberty." Chief Justice Story said: "In the code of laws established in Rhode Island we read for the first time since Constantine ascended the throne of the Caesars, the declaration that conscience should be free, and men should not be punished for worshipping God in the way they were persuaded He requires." Oscar S. Straus, in his life of Roger Williams, contests the Romanists' claim about Maryland and claims that Williams antedated Lord Baltimore. We know that a large majority of the settlers of Maryland were Protestants; that what Baltimore did was from expediency rather than principle; and that he was an immoral money-getter who never contributed a dollar to a church.*

Baptists have been forward in education in America. Brown University, the first college in the Middle States and in the front rank of American institutions of learning, was

---

*Since Catholics make so much out of the founding of Maryland, it should be remembered that twenty years before the occupation of Maryland the Baptists of England (1614) published a confession of faith in which they used this language: "We believe that the magistrate is not to meddle with religion or matters of conscience nor compel men to this or that form of religion, because Christ is the King and Law-giver of the church and the conscience." Then, again, the Maryland adventure was purely mercenary. Mr. E. D. Neil, after the most painstaking and accurate study of the original sources of this part of colonial history, characterizes Cecilius, second Lord Baltimore, as "one

founded by Baptists in 1764, and the charter requires that the president shall be a Baptist. The first real college in America for the higher education of women—Vassar—was founded by Matthew Vassar, a Baptist. Other colleges for women have since been founded, but "the primacy of Vassar is far more than chronological."

The literature of the world has been enriched by Baptist writers. Daniel DeFoe, the author of Robinson Crusoe; John Foster, the great essayist; John Howard, the philanthropist; John Milton, the great epic poet and statesman; and John Bunyan, the immortal dreamer, whose "Pilgrim's Progress" ranks next to the Bible in extent of its circulation, were all Baptists.

Milton began as a member of the Church of England, then became a strong Presbyterian,

whose whole life was passed in self-aggrandizement, first deserting Father White, then Charles I., and making friends of Puritans and republicans to secure the rentals of the province of Maryland, and never contributing a penny for a church or schoolhouse." Says Bacon: "Lord Baltimore may not have been a profound political philosopher nor a prophet of the coming era of religious liberty, but he was an adroit courtier, like his father before him, and he was a man of practical good sense engaged in an enormous land speculation in which his whole fortune was embarked, and he was not in the least disposed to allow his religious predilections to interfere with business."

then finding that Presbyterianism represented "as much of intolerance and tyranny as belonged to the Roman Church," he became an Independent, and theoretically a Baptist. He held the fundamental Baptist principle of separation of Church and State, rejected infant baptism, and contended that immersion in water is the proper form of baptism. Two quotations from his "Christian Doctrine" will suffice. "Infants are not to be baptized in as much as they are incompetent to receive instruction or to believe, or to enter into a covenant, or to promise or answer for themselves, or even to hear a word." "The bodies of believers, who engage themselves to pureness of life, are immersed in running water." Under the influence of Roger Williams he came out squarely and opposed interference of the State or civil magistrate in any way in matters of religious belief. He and John Bunyan, by the estimate of Lord Macaulay, were the two minds of the latter half of the seventeenth century which possessed the "imaginative faculty" in a very eminent degree. One produced "Paradise Lost"; the other, "Pilgrim's Progress." Differing in many respects they were alike in their dependence upon the word of God, and in their tenacity to Baptist principles. One sounded those principles "like a grand organ peal"; the other sounded them with the simplicity, unaffectedness, and persuasiveness of a singer of the soil.

It is a noteworthy fact that to the Baptists the world is indebted for the most popular national hymn of our language, "My Country, 'Tis of Thee." Baptists also wrote:

How Firm a Foundation; My Hope is Built; Jesus, Thou Art the Sinner's Friend; Awake, My Soul, in Joyful Lays; O, Could I Speak the Matchless Worth; Majestic Sweetness Sits Enthroned; Come, Humble Sinner, in Whose Breast; Did Christ O'er Sinners Weep? The Morning Light is Breaking; Take the Name of Jesus With You; Saviour, Thy Dying Love; Shall We Gather at the River? He Leadeth Me, O Blessed Thought; I Need Thee Every Hour; I Am So Glad that Our Father in Heaven; Almost Persuaded; Where is My Wandering Boy Tonight? On Jordan's Stormy Banks; Dare to be a Daniel; Blest Be the Tie that Binds; How Precious is the Book Divine; Lord, Dismiss Us With Thy Blessing; Come, Thou Fount of Every Blessing; Softly Fades the Twilight Ray; Come Holy Spirit, Heavenly Dove; Father, Whate'er of Earthly Bliss; My Jesus, I Love Thee; God, in the Gospel of His Son; O, Safe to the Rock That is Higher Than I; Go, Preach the Blest Salvation; Our Country's Voice is Pleading; Holy Bible,

Book Divine; Ye Christian Heralds, Go Proclaim; O Thou My Soul, Forget No More; More Holiness Give Me; Wonderful Words of Life; Whosoever Will; The Light of the World is Jesus; The Half Was Never Told; Bringing in the Sheaves.

W. H. Doane, a Baptist, wrote the music for many of our popular hymns, such as:

Pass Me Not, O Gentle Saviour; Near the Cross; I Am Thine, O Lord; 'Tis the Blessed Hour of Prayer; Some Sweet Day; Saviour More Than Life to Me; More Love to Thee, O Christ; Hide Me, Oh, My Saviour, Hide Me; Will Jesus Find Us Watching? What Shall the Harvest Be? Rescue the Perishing; To the Work.

Robert Lowry, a Baptist, wrote the musci for "Saviour, Thy Dying Love," and "We're Marching to Zion." "Coronation," the tune sung round the world, was written by Oliver Holden, a Baptist. These songs have smoothed more dying pillows and comforted more sorrowing hearts than all the philosophies from Plato to Bergson.

Baptists have an honorable history. Their record is clean upon the separation of Church and State. Having given to the United States religious freedom, at the cost of their property, their liberty, their good name, and their lives, it is their chief glory that, suffering all martyrdom themselves, they never yet have persecuted others.

Their place has ever been with the pioneers of humanity. On many a field of battle and of blood, the banner of civil and religious liberty has been borne aloft by Baptist hands. To them the two things supremely worth while are Religion and Liberty. These are closely akin. They are essential to the highest good of man. Joined in one word, Religious-Liberty, the perpetuity of each is guaranteed. The draft of the League of Nations read by President Wilson to the Peace Conference provided freedom of conscience or religion to the colonies of Central Africa. Baptists had, months before the war ended, petitioned that these rights be granted in every nation. We have come a long way from the days of oppression and have come through much tribulation. If our principles are now the possession, or aspiration, of all people who read and think, and our passionate love of liberty is the native air of this great land, and the growing sentiment of all lands, it is largely because these principles have been woven into the warp and woof of human thought by generations of heroic souls who held the Baptist faith.

A Mighty Present.

The legacies of the past have made the present rich and strong for us. Baptists have no extensive ecclesiastical appliances for gathering statistics and the figures do not show our full strength. However incomplete they may be, they are nevertheless very gratifying. The total number of Baptists in the world, according to the Baptist Year Book, is 8,070,762. Baptists of the world have increased 8,000 per cent. in one hundred and twenty-five years and they number one-twentieth of the Christian population of the earth. Government statistics for 1918 give us in the United States 58,913 churches, 43,656 ministers, and 7,213,922 members. We are second to the Methodists, with 7,-608,284, and every one in our figures represents a person who has reached the age of accountability. Our ministers exceed those of the Methodists by 1,405. Presbyterians number 2,171,601; Lutherans, 2,455,334; Episcopalians, 1,078,435; Disciples of Christ,

1,337,450; Church of Christ Scientists, 85,-
096; Unitarians, 71,110. Excepting the
Methodists, Baptists outnumber any three
denominations in the United States. From
1850 to 1900 the population of this country increased three and a half times, while
the Baptists increased almost six times.
Though the Episcopalians decreased 11,000
and the Disciples 35,000 in 1918, the Baptists increased 128,000, which was 50,000
more than the Catholics and 78,000 more
than the Methodists.

The stronghold of Baptists is the South.
The white members here number 2,593,249
and the colored 2,150,929. Their growth has
been rapid. In fifteen years Southern white
Baptists increased 61 per cent. in membership, 28 per cent. in churches, 105 per cent. in
baptisms, 353 per cent. in contributions to
missions, and 333 per cent. in total contributions.

Baptists outnumber any other Protestant
denomination in Alabama, Arkansas, Florida,
Georgia, Kentucky, Louisiana, Maine, Mississippi, North Carolina, South Carolina, Rhode
Island, Tennessee, Texas and Virginia; while

in each of the States of Alabama, Georgia, Mississippi, North Carolina, South Carolina and Virginia there are more members of Baptist churches than of all other denominations, including Roman Catholics. In the territory of the Southern Baptist Convention east of the Mississippi River Baptists have forty-five and seven-tenths per cent. of all membership in Christian denominations, and west of the river they have twenty-seven and five-tenths per cent., which is six and two-tenths per cent. more than the next largest evangelical denomination.

Baptists have the largest theological seminary in this country, and perhaps in the world. They have fifteen theological seminaries, one hundred and two colleges and universities, and one hundred and eighteen academies. Baptists have more money invested in property and endowments for educational institutions than any other religious body in the United States. The value of the property, including the endowments, is $99,608,885 and the total income of these educational institutions in 1917 was $7,266,015. We need carefully to note this and compare this in-

come with the total expenses of $8,087,215.
Here is an item that demands our most
serious attention. The income must be increased. There were 63,979 students in these
educational institutions and 2,371,750 volumes in the libraries. Baptists also have
their share of students in the State schools.

A Bright Future.

Our advance has always been greatest
where the people are the freest. The world
moves freedom's radiant way. The shackles
of oppression are falling from the peoples of
the earth. Men are coming into a conscious-
ness of their right to think, to decide, to act
for themselves, unawed by any arbitrary
power. Rulers are paying more attention
than ever to the masses. Democratic doctrines have turned the world upside down.
Even the Romanists, age-long hierarchists,
are talking democracy; uniformly advocates
of the union of Church and State, they are
professing belief in religious freedom. They
have "about-faced," and now professedly
look the way Baptists have always faced and
marched. We should welcome their change,

provided they "bring forth fruits meet for repentance." When order follows the holocaust of war we will confront an unparalleled opportunity. Just as America, by a self-sacrificing devotion to political democracy, has risen to the foremost place among nations, so may the Baptists by a no less ardent devotion to spiritual democracy, gain the hegemony among denominations.

This is no time for Baptists to be underlings. Possessors of a heritage which has enriched the world, they are to live lives worthy of their historic greatness. They dare not stand still and see a mighty stream flow by in channels cut by their own principles. Their place is on the bosom of the water, in the very middle of the stream. In order to do this at least two things are necessary.

(1) A new standard of giving. Our per capita contributions are shamefully small. We must be done with miserly contributions from the rich, and with no contributions from the many. The missionaries on the foreign field must be proportionate to our membership on the home field. Baptist institutions

of learning must be adequately equipped
and amply endowed. The pall of illiteracy
that hangs over America must be lifted and
our country illumined by the Baptist light.
The doctrine of stewardship must put a
dynamic in our doctrines of faith. We dare
not return to pre-war standards of giving to
the Kingdom of God. The war loosened
plethoric purse strings. How long will
periodic war be necessary to lower the high
blood pressure of material prosperity? Has
not this awful war been sufficient to instruct
us? The next few years will demonstrate.
Will our Christian men lapse into old habits
of ease and drop down to old standards of
giving? Then look out for another deluge!
Will they think world thoughts for the Kingdom of God? Will they render sacrificial
service for Christ? Will they support the
churches with millions as they have backed the
government with their cash and credit? To
put it bluntly: Do we love our souls as much
as we love our bodies? Will we do for Christ's
cause what we have done for our country?
Are we pre-eminently Christian?

(2) A new standard of living. The modern

mind is more concerned with life than doctrine. It conceives religion as an undertaking rather than an investigation. To be sure, one must know in order to teach, must believe before he speaks. Assuming that Baptists have this knowledge and conviction, let them become formative forces in all movements for moral betterment and social uplift. To say that the truth which Baptists hold is impaired by contact with life is a confession of weakness. The truth, like leaven, should permeate the lump, and assimilate instead of being assimilated. Other denominations need contact with the Baptists. Intimate acquaintance would promote understanding and heighten respect. By entering world affairs America is moulding them after her ideals. America might remain aloof in selfish geographical isolation. By so doing she possibly would preserve her own life; but what about those whom she could help? Leave them to discord and disunion and death? The conscience of the majority of Americans answers, "No!" Such a course ultimately would be fatal to ourselves and to them.

"Say not: 'It matters not to me
  My brother's weal is his behoof;'
For in this wondrous human web
  If his life's warp, your life's woof.
Woven together are the threads,
  And he and you are on one loom;
For good or ill, for glad or sad,
  Your lives must share a common doom."

The largest mission and brightest future of the Baptists lie in serving God by enriching the lives of men. Jesus defined this mission in one sentence: "I am come that they might have life, and that they might have it more abundantly." A denomination must so serve that those whom it reaches shall have a fuller, diviner life. The denomination which points out that the high road to the betterment of the world lies through moral principles rather than legal enactments; which preserves the mass by proclaiming the inexpressible value of the person; which acts as the mentor of the national conscience by reflecting with faultless precision the conscience of the individual; which preaches a gospel of industrial and social repentance; which breaks down the middle wall of partition between classes and reveals the meaning of brotherhood and love;

which has the spirit of self-sacrifice and will-
ingness to lose its own life for Christ; that is
the denomination to whom the future belongs.
Such a denomination makes a new earth
wherein dwelleth righteousness.

"God grant us wisdom in these coming days,
  And eyes unsealed, that we clear visions see
  Of that new world that He would have us build,
  To life's ennoblement and His high ministry.

"God give us sense—God-sense of Life's new needs,
  And souls aflame with new-born chivalries;
  To cope with those black growths that foul the ways,
  To cleanse our poisoned founts with God-born
      energies.

"To pledge our souls to nobler, loftier life;
  To win the world to His fair sanctities;
  To bind the nations in a pact of peace,
  And free the Soul of Life for finer loyalties.

"Not since Christ died upon His lonely cross,
  Has time such prospects held of Life's new birth;
  Not since the world of chaos first was born,
  Has man so clearly visaged hope of a new earth.

"Not of our own might can we hope to rise
  Above the ruts and soilures of the past,
  But, with His help who did the first earth build,
  With hearts courageous we may fairer build this
      last."

II.

THEIR DISTINGUISHING BELIEFS.

"It seemed good to me also, having traced the course of all things accurately from the first, to write unto thee in order . . . that thou mightest know the certainty concerning the things wherein thou wast instructed." Lu. 1:3, 4, R. V.

"But sanctify in your hearts Christ as Lord; being ready always to give answer to every man that asketh you a reason concerning the hope that is in you." 1 Peter 3:15.

Baptists are glad to hold many doctrines in common with other Christians. Among these are the Inspiration of the Scriptures; the Doctrine of the Trinity; the Ruin Wrought by Sin; Salvation Through Christ, and the Future Rewards of the Righteous and Punishment of the Wicked. These are equally dear to us and to Christian friends of other denominations.

But our separate existence is to be explained and justified by our belief in certain important principles which are either not held, or not held so tenaciously and consistently by others. Dr. J. L. M. Curry, with peculiar clearness says: "No religious denomination has a moral right to a separate existence unless it differs essentially from others. Ecclesiastical differences ought always to spring from profound doctrinal differences. To divide Christians, except for reasons of great import, is criminal schism. Sects are justified only for matters of conscience growing out of clear Scriptural precepts or inevitable logical inference. Human speculation, tradition, authority of pope, or council, or synod, or conference, or legislature, is no proper basis for an organization of Christians. Nothing short of the truth of revelation, the authoritative force of God's word, rising above mere prejudice, or passion, or caprice, can justify a distinct church organization."

By distinctive principles is meant those tenets which distinguish us from other people. Let me prepare the way for a statement of these principles by disclaiming as distinctive the three doctrines which others consider as constituting our distinctness. Two of these doctrines are held by us and one sometimes erroneously charged to us. (1) Immersion only is baptism. This is held by Baptists, but not by them alone. The Disciples so believe and practice. The Greek, or Eastern Church, has always practiced immersion and its present communion numbering over 70,-000,000 is immersed. Furthermore, immersion is not uncommon among Protestants. (2) Baptism is necessary to salvation. This has never been a tenet of the Baptists. They are the only people in the world who hold exactly the opposite, namely, that salvation must precede baptism. (3) "Close communion." Far from being a distinguishing doctrine of the Baptists, the principle underlying "close communion" and out of which it grows is held by all denominations. All agree that baptism comes before communion in the New Testament order. Roman Catholics, Episcopalians, Presbyterians, Lutherans and Methodists baptize their babes directly after they are born, but do not give them the communion for years. Why do they always baptize first if baptism does not come before the communion? To be exact, we should say, "participation" and "Lord's Supper" instead of "communion."

Having cleared the way by disclaiming number two as a doctrine of the Baptists and by saying numbers one and three are held in common with certain other Christians, those doctrines that are distinctive with us may now be stated.

1. We believe that the New Testament is the sole and sufficient rule of faith and practice.

2. We believe in individual responsibility to God for the performance of duty.

3. We believe that a church is a body of baptized believers, equal in rank and privilege, administering its own affairs under the headship of Jesus Christ.

Perhaps some of my Baptist brethren will think I have omitted something. Wait until these statements are developed and you will find that every tenet which characterizes us is included in these three statements. Perhaps some one of my fellow Christians among other denominations will think that I have stated principles which they hold as well as ourselves. Await the expansion of the thought and you will see that no people interpret and practice these principles as we do. We will consider them in the order of their statement.

The New Testament the Only Authority.

The New Testament is the only law of Christianity. The Old Testament is equally the word of God, but it was typical and is fulfilled in the New. It was the schoolmaster to lead us to Christ. Now we have Christ, who is our only law-giver and the only Lord of the conscience.

Baptists do not go to the Old but to the New Testament to find the laws of the church and its institutions. Circumcision was practiced in the Old Testament, but had no substitute in the New. We deny that the Christian Church should baptize infants because they were circumcised under the old law. Circumcision is too broad for baptism in that it included servants and too narrow in that it excluded females. If baptism was typified by circumcision it must be administered either to the actual or the spiritual seed of Abraham. It could not be his *actual* seed, since females are excluded. It could not be his *spiritual* seed, since all other nations are excluded. Therefore circumcision could not typify baptism. Such was Dr. B. H. Carroll's unanswerable argument on this point. Paul could have settled the annoying circumcision controversy by saying "Baptism has taken the place of circumcision." He never said it. We believe that the New Testament is a sufficient rule for the Christian life. Creeds and decrees of councils have no binding authority. The believer has his supreme and absolute guide in the New Testament illumined by the Holy Spirit.

Someone will say, for example, that he believes immersion was practiced and commanded by Jesus, but he thinks the church has a right to change the mode. Here is where the Baptist's position on the place and purpose of the New Testament makes him part company with all who so hold. Jesus is absolute Lord. The church has no right to undo what Christ has done. Its mission is to carry out what he has commanded. When the Presbyterians tell us that this is a principle of their denomination as well as of the Baptists, we ask them for the authority in the Scriptures for sprinkling and for infant baptism. By practicing both or either they invalidate their claim.

Furthermore, it is a serious matter to add to the things commanded. To those who keep more than two sacraments, or teach sacerdotalism, or observe an elaborate ritual, or possess an intricate and extensive form of government we say, "You have added to the law which is sole and sufficient. You have done that which is distinctly forbidden." "I testify unto every man that heareth the words of the prophecy of this book, if any man shall add unto them, God shall add unto him the plagues which are written in this book." You dare not *subtract from* by changing the mode of baptism. You dare not *add to* by multiplying the rites or ritual. As my beloved Bible teacher at Baylor University used to say, "*All* the New Testament is the Law of Christianity. The New Testament is *all* the Law of Christianity. The New Testament will *always* be the Law of Christianity."

Individual Responsibility.

This separates the individual from family, friends, government and all, and brings him face to face with his Maker. "To his own Master he standeth or falleth." "So, then, every one of us must give account of himself to God." The first preacher in the New Testament proclaimed the blessed doctrine of individualism. If we listen we may hear the clarion voice of John the Baptist ringing from the regions of Jordan—breaking the silence of four hundred years—crying, "Think not to say within yourselves, we have Abraham to our father. Behold the axe is laid at the root of the tree and every tree that bringeth not forth fruit is hewn down and cast into the fire."

Individual responsibility means freedom of choice. Freedom to *read* the Bible; freedom to *interpret* the Bible; freedom to *approach* God; freedom to *serve* God. The Baptists would have a Bible within the possession of every one who wants it. They would say, "Read, interpret, and decide for yourself." They would not, for any consideration, baptize unconscious infants or force their own children into their churches. Yea, they say to their most dearly beloved, "Go where the New Testament leads you." Therefore every member of a Baptist church secured that membership upon his own initiative. Not one was brought in unconsciously or unwillingly.

Nor do we believe in the intervention of priests between the soul and God. According to our belief, all believers are priests and may directly confess their sins, express their praise, and ask for guidance. By reason of their belief in individualism, Baptists have ever been the opponents of the union of Church and State and the champions of Religious Liberty. They were such not by accident, but by the necessity of their principles. Freedom of conscience is a corollary of individualism. Considered historically, this tenet belongs to us alone.

At the beginning of the struggle we stood against the world with nothing but the word of God on our side. Our contention is based upon such Scriptures as, "Shadrach, Meshach and Abednego answered and said to the king,

O, Nebuchadnezzar, we are not careful to answer thee in this matter. If it be so, our God whom we serve is able to deliver us from the burning fiery furnace, and He will deliver us out of thine hand, O king. But if not, be it known unto thee, O king, that we will not serve thy gods, nor worship the golden image which thou hast set up." Dan. 3:16, 18.

"Tell us therefore, What thinkest thou? Is it lawful to give tribute unto Caesar, or not? But Jesus perceived their wickedness, and said, Why tempt ye me, ye hypocrites? Shew me the tribute money. And they brought unto Him a penny. And He saith unto them, Whose is this image and superscription? They said unto him, Caesar's. Then saith He unto them, Render therefore unto Caesar the things which are Caesar's; and unto God the things that are God's. When they had heard these words, they marvelled, and left Him, and went their way." Matt. 22:17-22.

"And they called them, and commanded them not to speak at all nor teach in the name of Jesus. But Peter and John answered and said unto them, Whether it be right in the sight of God to hearken unto you more than unto God, judge ye. For we cannot but speak the things which we have seen and heard." Acts 4:18-20.

"Then Peter and the other apostles answered and said, We ought to obey God rather than men." Acts 5:29.

Baptists contend that there can be no coercion in matters pertaining to conscience. God Himself does not force men. Religion is purely voluntary. The civil power can make a nation of hypocrites and infidels, but not one Christian. What havoc has been wrought by a disregard of this principle! Calvin burned Servetus at the stake near Geneva and Melancthon approved the crime. Luther persecuted the Baptists of Germany. Louis XIV. revoked the Edict of Nantes, closed all the Protestant churches, and outlawed the Huguenots. No sooner had the Netherlands repelled Philip II. and the Catholic persecution than the Protestants turned upon each other. The Calvinists, led by Prince Maurice, executed the venerable John Barneveldt; and condemned to life imprisonment her greatest historian, Hugo Grotius, upon the charge that he supported *religious toleration*. England kept John Bunyan twelve years in prison because he would not conform to the established worship. The most shameful chapter of American history is that which records the persecution of Baptists for conscience's sake. In Massachusetts, Obadiah Holmes was whipped on Boston Common. Clark was imprisoned and Roger Williams was banished. In Connecticut the choicest lands of the Baptists were sold to build a church and support a ministry in which they did not believe. In Virginia they imprisoned Lewis Craig in Spotsylvania, William Webber in Chesterfield, James Greenwood in King and Queen, John Shackleford in Essex, John Waller in Middlesex, and John Ireland at Culpeper for preaching the gospel. Yea, they confiscated the property of Baptists to support a worldly and profligate ministry of the establishment. The Baptists have ever fearlessly denounced the unholy union of Church and State and proclaimed the right of every man to worship God as he chooses. Their principles will not allow them to persecute. They have never shed any blood but their own, nor can they ever shed blood if they have the power. The moment one began to persecute, that moment he would cease to be a Baptist.

A New Testament Church.

It is certain that Christ and his apostles baptized. It is equally certain that they baptized only *believers*. The church is for saved people. John the Baptist and Jesus made disciples before they baptized them. John 4:1. Jesus commanded us to be made disciples before we baptize. "The Lord added to them day by day those that were saved." Acts 2:47. "Believers were the more added unto the Lord, multitudes both of men and women." Acts 5:14. The churches are addressed thus, "But ye are washed, but ye are sanctified, but ye are justified in the name of the Lord Jesus." 1 Cor. 6:11. "And you hath he quickened who were dead in trespasses and sins." Eph. 2:1. They are also called, "beloved of God," "sanctified in Christ Jesus," "saints and faithful brethren in Christ." There is absolutely no evidence that baptism was administered except upon a voluntary profession of faith. If it is permissible to take into the church *one* unconverted, then it is permissible to take into the church *all* unconverted and thereby to have churches composed entirely of unbelieving sinners. We demand repentance and faith before baptism.

The household baptisms furnish no evidence that any but believers were baptized. There are five of these households mentioned in the Acts and Epistles. Examine them. (1) Cornelius—Acts 10:44-48, 11:14. His household evidently consisted of believers, for it is written that he "feared God *with all his house*." Moreover, the record states, "the Holy Spirit fell on all them *which heard the word*" and that they began to "speak with *tongues* and *magnify* God." Surely infants could not have performed any of these four functions. (2) Crispus—Acts 18:8; 1 Cor. 1:14. It reads like the account of Cornelius: "Crispus, the ruler of the synagogue, believed in the Lord *with all his house*." (3) Stephanas —1 Cor. 1:16; 16:15f. His household are described as "*the first fruits* of Achaia"; that is, they were the earliest converts. Further-more, five years after their baptism Paul wrote of them: "They have set themselves *to minister* unto the saints," and he exhorted the Corinthians to "be *in subjection* unto such." Could children six years old be spoken of in such language? (4) The jailer—Acts 16:31-34. We are informed that Paul and Silas "spake the word of the Lord unto him, *with all that were in his house.*" Infants could not be included among the auditors, and it is guess work to suppose they were afterwards baptized. (5) Lydia—Acts 16:13-15, 40. To get infants baptized here one must assume three things: (1) Lydia had a husband; (2) she had infant children; (3) these infants were baptized. Those are bold assumptions without a scintilla of proof. *"My house"* would indicate that she did not have a hus-band. She was a business woman with ser-vants. Before leaving Philippi, the Apostles paid her a farewell visit; the account reads, "when they had seen the *brethren* they com-forted them and departed." The "brethren" were members of her household and they were old enough to be "comforted" or exhorted.

They must have been persons of intelligence. A close reading of the Scriptures will disclose that acts and functions are described in every household of which infants are incapable. The Holy Spirit superintended the record so as to preserve believers' baptism. Dr. Archibald Alexander, distinguished Presbyterian scholar and president of Hampden-Sidney College, in 1796 communicated to the Presbytery his determination to give up infant baptism and avowed that only two considerations kept him back from joining the Baptists. The first was an argument from the "universal prevalence of infant baptism as early as the fourth and fifth centuries"; and the second was, "that if the Baptists are right, they are the only Christian church on earth." The Romanists object to the Baptists on similar grounds.

Infant baptism does not appear in Scripture at all and is not mentioned in history until shortly before the close of the second century, when Tertullian at Carthage opposed it as an innovation. The belief that baptism was essential to salvation and that infants dying unbaptized were lost facilitated the growth

of infant baptism; but no one advocated it
before Augustine (354-430). The heresy
spread and became the prolific parent of an
unregenerated church membership, of the
servitude of the individual to an institution,
of the union of Church and State and of persecution for conscience sake. It remains the
bulwark of Romanism and the most insur-
mountable barrier to Christian union.

The New Testament churches were independent and self-governing. The highest
court was the church. Matt. 18:15-18. Its
decisions were final. Each church is a court
and there is none higher. No general body
can dictate to the local church. Such general bodies are composed of messengers from
co-operating churches and are purely advisory.
The churches of the New Testament were
certainly independent organizations recogniz-
ing Jesus as their law-giver. The only earthly
bond of union was a common faith and life
and work. They were the only ecclesiastical
bodies. That each church governed its own
affairs is evident from Matt. 18:17. "And
if he shall neglect to hear them, tell it unto
the church: but if he neglect to hear the

church, let him be unto thee as an heathen man and a publican." 1 Cor. 5:3-5. "For I verily, as absent in body, but present in spirit, have judged already, as though I were present, concerning him that hath so done this deed, in the name of our Lord Jesus Christ, *when ye are gathered together*, and my spirit, with the power of our Lord Jesus Christ, to deliver such an one unto Satan for the destruction of the flesh, that the spirit may be saved in the day of the Lord Jesus." Acts 15:22. "Then pleased it the apostles and elders, *with the whole church*, to send chosen men of their own company to Antioch with Paul and Barnabas." 2 Cor. 8:19. "And not that only, but who was *also chosen of the churches* to travel with us with this grace, which is administered by us to the glory of the same Lord, and declaration of your ready mind."

To particularize: each church had absolute control over its own membership. The church *received* members. "Him that is weak in the faith receive ye, but not to doubtful disputations." Rom. 14:1. One joins a church for fellowship, worship and service. The members have a right to say whether or not they think he will promote that fellowship, worship and service. Otherwise, inharmonious and discordant elements may get into the same church.

The church *withdrew* fellowship from members for cause. "Now we command you, brethren, in the name of our Lord Jesus Christ, that ye withdraw yourselves from every brother that walketh disorderly, and not after the tradition which he received of us." 2 Thess. 3:6. It is absurd to vote one out if you do not vote him in. Once more, if the pastor, or any certain class, has a right to take a member in, he has a right to turn him out. Under the Baptist polity the whole church receives him and the same church excludes, for cause.

It *restored* to fellowship upon repentance. "Brethren, if a man be overtaken in a fault, ye which are spiritual restore such an one in the spirit of meekness: considering thyself, lest thou also be tempted." Gal. 6:1. The general congregation votes to receive back into the fellowship the erring member who has been reclaimed.

Baptists find no authority in the Bible for

one man being the head of an ecclesiastical organization. Peter never knew he was a pope, nor did the other apostles. He was a fallible, married man. He did not appoint the successor to Judas. He spoke to the Christians as to his equals and they nominated. James was pastor and presided over the Jerusalem council and exerted the greatest influence. Paul withstood Peter to his face. Papal aggression began with Leo about the middle of the fifth century, culminated with Hildebrand about the middle of the eleventh century, and reached its climax of absurdity at the Vatican Council in 1870 by the formal declaration of papal infallibility. Our Saviour condemned the custom of giving one superiority over others. "And he said unto them, The kings of the Gentiles exercise lordship over them; and they that exercise authority upon them are called benefactors. But ye shall not be so: but he that is greatest among you, let him be as the younger; and he that is chief, as he that doth serve." Luke 22:25, 26. "But be ye not called Rabbi: for one is your Master, even Christ; and all ye are brethren. And call no man

your Father upon the earth: for one is your
Father, which is in heaven." Matt. 23:8, 9.
Even in the local church no one lords it over
God's heritage. Bishops were not "over"
but among them as the Revised Version cor-
rectly translates Acts 20:28, and the same
translation should be made of 1 Thess. 5:12.
The only one over the church was the Lord
Jesus.

We understand that elder, bishop and pastor were terms designating those having care
of the local churches and were used interchangeably, the same person being called
elder, bishop or pastor, according to the view
taken of his office. "Elders" is the term
used in Acts 20:17 to designate the Ephesian
presbyters, and in Acts 20:28 they are called
"bishops." Now, "bishop" means overseer
or pastor. So we have the words used interchangeably in one chapter referring to the
same persons. Elder and bishop are also
used interchangeably in Titus 1:5, 7. See
also 1 Peter 2:25 and 5:5. The words de-
scribe different functions of the same office;
three departments of work in one office.
Viewing the church as a force of laborers, they

have an "episcopos," overseer, to superin-
tend their activities; viewing the church as a
flock, they have a shepherd, pastor, to shepherd the sheep; viewing the church as an
assembly, they have an elder, a ruler, to pre-
side.

New Testament churches selected their
own officers and messengers. This appears
from Acts 1:21-26, where Matthias was selected by all of the remaining apostles and
the women and the brothers of Jesus as the
successor of Judas. The "multitude of the
disciples" selected the seven (Acts 6:2f)
who served as deacons. In commenting upon
Acts 14:23, Meyer says, "Paul and Barnabas
chose by vote presbyters for them, i. e.,
they *conducted their selection by vote in the
churches.*" The verb used here is to extend
the hand and signifies properly to elect or
vote by extending the hand. The choice of
companions to attend the apostles in the name
of the communities was left to the churches
themselves. We read "Who was appointed
by the churches to travel with us" (2 Cor.
8:19). The local church, then, chose its
officers who were of but two classes, viz.,

Bishops and Deacons. See Phil. 1:1 and 1 Tim. 3:1, 8, where the deacons are named immediately after the bishops, "which excludes the idea of any intermediate order."

To-day, Baptist churches have absolute control over their affairs and elect their own officers as did those in the days of the apostles. If we were to admit that we had no form of church government laid down in the New Testament we should still believe in our form of local government, because it accords with our sense of freedom and justice. As a minister, it seems, I should not like for the place and time of my pastorate to be determined by another man. As a layman, I should want some voice and vote in determining who was to be my pastor and how long he was to remain.

Baptist principles are founded upon God's word and are in accord with the innate sense of freedom in the human heart. Our success is conditioned upon our loyalty to these principles in the spirit of the Master.

III

THE INITIAL CHRISTIAN ORDINANCE.

"Buried with him in baptism, wherein also ye are risen with him through the faith of the operation of God, who hath raised him from the dead."   Col. 2:12.

"Therefore we are buried with him by baptism into death; that like as Christ was raised up from the dead by the glory of the Father, even so we also should walk in newness of life."   Rom. 6:4.

Doctrinal preaching has an important place in the dissemination of the gospel. Such preaching should not be dessicated or acerbating. When neglected, the result is seen in a membership of lax and unsettled views. "Speaking the truth in love" should be our motto as we calmly and soberly endeavor to show that the Baptists are correct in their practice of immersion and that only.

I. The Greek word translated baptize means immerse.

Proof.—All the authorities cited are Pedo-Baptists.

1. Lexicons.

(*a*) Liddell & Scott—"Baptism, to dip in or under water." Classical.

(*b*) Thayer—"Baptism, to dip repeatedly, to immerse, submerge. An immersion in water." A Greek English Lexicon of the New Testament, date 1887.

(*c*) Sophocles—"Baptize, to dip, to immerse, to sink. . . . . There is no evidence that Luke and Paul and the other writers of the New Testament put upon the verb meanings not recognized by the Greeks." "Greek Lexicon of the Roman and Byzantine Periods," date 1870.

2. Encyclopedias.

(*a*) Kitto's—"Baptism, that is dipping or immersion."

(*b*) Britannica—"The word is derived from the Greek to dip, or wash."

3. Dictionaries.

(*a*) Smith—"Baptism properly and literally means immersion."

(*b*) Marcus Dods—"To use Pauline language, his old man is dead and buried in the water, and he rises from his cleansing grave a new man. The full significance of the rite would have been lost had immersion not been practiced." "Dictionary of Christ and the Gospels," by Hastings. (1906-1908.)

4. Histories.

Fisher—"The ordinary mode of baptism was by immersion."

5. History.

(*a*) Greek church, old and knowing the language, practices immersion only.

(*b*) The earliest case of sprinkling on record is that of Novation, 250 A. D., and it originated in a baptism of the sick, and this was not accepted by all as valid. Novation recovered and became a minister, but some always opposed his eligibility to the office on the ground that he had never been baptized. One can readily see that a belief in baptismal regeneration was the cause for sprinkling one who was thought to be dying.

6. Fathers.

Tertullian—"The law of immersion has been imposed, and the form has been prescribed."

7. Commentators and Translators.

(*a*) John Calvin (Presbyterian) — "The word 'baptize' signifies to immerse. It is certain that immersion was the practice of the primitive church."

(*b*) Luther (Lutheran)—"Baptism is a Greek word, and may be translated 'Immerse.' I would have those who are to be baptized to be altogether dipped."

(*c*) John Wesley (Methodist) — "Buried with him by baptism—alluding to the ancient manner of baptizing by immersion."

(*d*) Wall (Episcopalian)—"Immersion was in all probability the way in which our blessed Saviour, and for certain the way by which the ancient Christians received their baptism."

(*e*) Brenner (Catholic)—"For thirteen hundred years was baptism an immersion of the person under water."

Conclusion.—By seven different methods and from fourteen anti-Baptist authorities I have shown that the Greek word means immerse, and was so interpreted and practiced by early Christians. It is a rule in court practice that a person cannot impeach his own witness, and yet our Pedo-baptist friends would be forced to that before they could overthrow the Baptist position.

II. There is no instance in the Bible where God ever commanded any one to sprinkle pure water upon anything for any purpose. Ask the Old Testament for the authority for sprinkling; it replies, "It is not in me." Ask the New Testament; it replies, "It is not in me." This is shown by an examination of all the passages in original or translation in which reference is made to the idea of sprinkling. Only two Hebrew words in the Old Testament are translated sprinkle in our version of the Scriptures—*Zah-rak* and *Nah-zah*.

1. *Nah-zah*—twenty-four times in the Old Testament.

(*a*) Used of sprinkling blood, twelve times. Lev. 4:6, 17; 5:9; 6:27, twice; 16:14 twice, and verses 15 and 19; Num. 19:4; 2 Ki. 9:33; Is. 63:3. Blood is the object of the verb in every case.

(*b*) Used of sprinkling blood and oil, twice. Lev. 8:30; Ex. 19:21.

(*c*) Used of sprinkling blood and water mingled, twice. Lev. 14:7, 51.

(*d*) Used of sprinkling blood and oil, three times. Lev. 8:11; 14:16, 27.

(*e*) Used of sprinkling blood, ashes and water mingled, four times. Num. 19:18, 19, 21. "And a clean person shall take hyssop, and dip it in the water, and sprinkle it upon the tent, and upon all the vessels, and upon the persons that were there, and upon him that touched a bone, or one slain, or one dead, or a grave:

And the clean person shall sprinkle upon the unclean on the third day, and on the seventh day; and on the seventh day he shall purify himself, and wash his clothes, and bathe himself in water, and shall be clean at even.

And it shall be a perpetual statute unto them, that he that sprinkleth the water of separation shall wash his clothes; and he that toucheth the water of separation shall be unclean until even."

(*f*) Once in Is. 52:15. So shall he astonish or startle (Revised Version) many nations.

2. *Zah-rah.*—Thirty-five times in the Old Testament.

(*a*) Used of sprinkling blood, twenty-five times. Ex. 24:6, 8; 29:16, 20; Lev. 1:5, 11;

3:2, 8, 13; 7:2; 8:19, 24; 9:12, 18; 17:6; Num. 18:17; 2 Ki. 16:13, 15; 2 Chron. 29:22 (three times); 30:16; 35:11; Ezek. 43:18.

(*b*) Used of sprinkling ashes and water mingled, twice. Num. 19:13, 20.

(*c*) Used of scattering small solid substances, seven times. (1) Dust, 2 Chron. 34:4; Job 2:12; (2) Ashes, Ex. 9:8, 10; (3) Seeds, Is. 28:25; (4) Gray hairs, Hosea 7:9; (5) Coals of fire, Ezek, 10:2.

(*d*) Ezek. 36:25—"Then will I sprinkle clean water upon you and ye shall be clean: from all your filthiness and from all your idols, will I cleanse you."

Here it is used figuratively of cleansing water. Consider the

(1) General usage. The water of purification was always clean as uncontaminated and cleansing.

(2) God is the subject of the sentence and no one contends that it literally means God will sprinkle in showers and dews.

(3) National custom. A figure is not to be ascribed to an assumed custom when it can be explained on known customs as well. Water of purification is referred to in Lev.

15:19, 30. "And if a woman have an issue and her issue in her flesh be blood, she shall be put apart seven days; and whosoever toucheth her shall be unclean until the even."

"And the priest shall offer the one for a sin offering, and the other for a burnt offering; and the priest shall make an atonement for her before the Lord for the issue of her uncleanness." By comparing Num. 19:17 we learn what the water of purification was. It was the ashes of a red heifer mixed with running water.

There is no case, or even a hint, where sprinkling of simple water ever occurred. The Jews did many things not commanded, but not this, and if they had done this it would not be binding on us.

3. If sprinkling as now practiced has any countenance from God, it must be in the New Testament; but let us see—The only word in the New Testament to denote sprinkling is *rantizo*. It is always used of blood.

(*a*) Heb. 9:13, 19, 21; 10:22. (13) "For if the *blood* of bulls and of goats, and the ashes of an heifer *sprinkling* the unclean, sanctifieth to the purifying of the flesh." (19) "For

when Moses had spoken every precept to all
the people according to the law, he took the
blood of calves and of goats, with water, and
scarlet wool, and hyssop, and sprinkled both
the book, and all the people." (21) "Moreover he sprinkled with blood both the taber-
nacle, and all the vessels of the ministry."
10:22. "Let us draw near with a true heart
in full assurance of faith, having our hearts
sprinkled from an evil conscience, and our
bodies washed with pure water." Blood is
expressed in all passages but the last and must
be supplied here to get the correct meaning.

(b) *Rantismos* (sprinkling) occurs twice
in New Testament and refers to blood.

Heb. 12:24. "And to Jesus the mediator
of the new covenant, and to the blood of
sprinkling, that speaketh better things than
that of Abel."

1 Peter 1:2. "Elect according to the fore-
knowledge of God the Father, through sanctification of the Spirit, unto obedience and
sprinkling of the blood of Jesus Christ: Grace
unto you, and peace, be multiplied."

(c) *Proschusis*—translated sprinkling, occurs once and refers to blood. "Through

faith he kept the passover, and the sprinkling of blood, lest he that destroyed the first-born should touch them." Heb. 11:28.

Sprinkling clear water is not commanded, mentioned or hinted. This is unaccountable if God intended it as an ordinance. There is a great deal of sprinkling in the Old Testament, but none of clear water. Sprinkling of blood is all that is alluded to in the New Testament.

4. Pouring occurs in the New Testament twenty-four times, but is never of water, nor is *baptizo* ever so translated. In four instances some form of the verb *ballo* is used and in twenty instances some form of the verb *eccheo*.

(1) Of wine, Mt. 9:17; Mk. 2:22; (2) Emptying the changer's money, Jno. 2:15; (3) Outpouring of the Holy Spirit, Acts 2:17, 18, 33; 10:45; Tit. 3:6; (4) Shedding of blood, Acts 22:20; Rom. 3:15; Rev. 16:6; (5) Oil and wine upon wounds of man who fell among thieves, Lk. 10:34; (6) Pouring ointment on the Saviour's head, Mt. 26:7, 12; Mk. 14:3; (7) Pouring water into a basin to wash his disciples' feet, Jno. 13:5; (8) Of outpouring

of the vials of wrath, Rev. 16:1, 2, 3, 4, 8, 10, 12 and 17.   There is no case in the New Testament in which water was poured upon any one.   Neither sprinkling nor pouring is in the Bible, and hence cannot be a form of Christian baptism.

III. Jesus Christ was certainly immersed by John the Baptist and his apostles practiced the same mode—

1. Baptism of Jesus. The account is in five places. Mt. 3:13-17; Mk. 1:9-11; Lk. 3:21; Rom. 6:3-5; Col. 2:12. I quote them:

"Then cometh Jesus from Galilee to Jordan unto John, to be baptized of him.   But John forbade him, saying, I have need to be baptized of thee, and comest thou to me?   And Jesus answering said unto him, Suffer it to be so now: for thus it becometh us to fulfill all righteousness.   Then he suffered him. And Jesus, when he was baptized, went up straightway out of the waters and lo, the heavens were opened unto him, and he saw the Spirit of God descending like a dove, and lighting upon him: and lo a voice from heaven, saying, This is my beloved Son, in whom I am well pleased."   Mt. 3:13-17.

"And it came to pass in those days that Jesus came from Nazareth of Galilee, and was baptized of John in Jordan. And straightway coming up out of the water he saw the heavens opened, and the Spirit like a dove descending upon him: And there came a voice from heaven saying, Thou art my beloved Son, in whom I am well pleased." Mk. 1:9-11.

"Now when all the people were baptized, it came to pass, that Jesus also being baptized, and praying, the heaven was opened: And the Holy Ghost descended in a bodily shape like a dove upon him, and a voice came from heaven, which said, Thou art my beloved Son; in thee I am well pleased." (Lk. 3:21f.)

"Know ye not, that so many of us as were baptized into Jesus Christ were baptized into his death? Therefore we are buried with him by baptism into death: that like as Christ was raised up from the dead by the glory of the Father, even so we also should walk in newness of life. For if we have been planted together in the likeness of his death, we shall be also in the likeness of his resurrection." (Rom. 6:3-5.)

"Buried with him in baptism, wherein also ye are risen with him through the faith of the operation of God, who hath raised him from the dead." (Col. 2:12.) Note (*a*) In what— River; (*b*) Came up out of; (*c*) Buried; (*d*) Risen in baptism with Christ. Such terms are appropriate to immersion only. (Col. 2:12.)

2. John's continual practice. "In Aenon near to Salim, because there was much water there." (Jno. 3:23.) He received his name from his custom of baptizing.

3. Philip and the Eunuch. "And as they went on their way, they came unto a certain water; and the eunuch said, See, here is water; what doth hinder me to be baptized? And Philip said, If thou believest with all thine heart, thou mayest. And he answered, and said, I believe that Jesus Christ is the Son of God. And he commanded the chariot to stand still; and THEY went down BOTH into the water, BOTH PHILIP AND THE EUNUCH; and he baptized him. And when they were come up out of the water the Spirit of the Lord caught away Philip, that the eunuch saw him no more: and he went on his

way rejoicing." (Acts 8:36-39.) The four
duals in verse 38 are significant. This is the
most minute description of the ordinance in
the Bible and leaves no doubt as to the mode.

IV. The baptism of 3,000 at Pentecost and
of the Jailer present no difficulty.

1. Case of the 3,000. It is objected that
they could not have been immersed.

(a) Scripture does not say all were baptized
in one day.

(b) The twelve apostles, each baptizing
thirty-two an hour, could have baptized
3,076 in eight hours. I have baptized a
large number of persons at one time and it required less than a minute to a person. It is
not at all taxing upon the strength of the
minister.

(c) Almost certainly the seventy sent out
by Jesus aided in the baptism.

(d) It is common in history for 3,000 to be
baptized in one day. Chrysostom baptized
3,000 in Constantinople 16th of April A. D.,
404. St. Patrick of Ireland immersed 120,000
during his life. In Madras Confederacy in
1878 six missionaries immersed in nine hours,

two baptizing at a time, 2,222. On December 28, 1890, they baptized 1,671 more.

2. Case of jailer, Acts 16:29. Opponents of immersion say he was in the jail and there was no place for immersion. A careful reading of the passage shows—

(*a*) His conversion did not take place in prison.

(*b*) His baptism did not take place in the prison house.

(*c*) Paul perhaps carried him to the river near by.

(*d*) Persons have been immersed in prison. Men are immersed in the penitentiary at Richmond every year. These objections are superficial.

V. Certain fundamental principles in law to be remembered are—

1. Words of law are to be understood in their ordinary sense. The ordinary meaning of baptize is to immerse. Dr. Broadus translated the Greek word immerse in every place in the New Testament and it fit the sense. Try this with sprinkle or pour and the result is ridiculous. *Eccheo* (pour) and *rantizo*

(sprinkle) are never used as synonyms for *baptizo*.

2. You cannot depart from the words of the law. Departure means to disregard the law. If one admits immersion as the New Testament mode but says the mode is unimportant, we say you have no right to change the law.

3. Where law is uncertain, there is no law. If we cannot know the prescribed form of baptism, then we have no form at all.

4. It availeth nothing if you know what is to be done and do not know *how* it is to be done. Uncertainty about the mode of baptism practically destroys baptism itself.

5. A law, when it expresses one thing, excludes everything else. Agents buying horses for the government by specification cut out all animals that do not come up to the requirements as to height and size, no matter how pretty such animals are.

6. The law requires absolute obedience. The registration law says all qualified voters must register by a certain time on a certain day. One coming thirty minutes after the hour would not be allowed to register.

(*a*) Baptism is a matter of much importance. It has been commanded by the Lord. The use of water is in one particular way. The Baptist principle is "obedience to Christ."

(*b*) The meaning is obscured if you change the mode. Death, burial and resurrection are not set forth by any other mode.

(*c*) Obedience is the test of love.   "If ye love me keep my commandments; he that hath my commandments and keepeth them, he it is that loveth me." The proper mode is of such importance that Judson was immersed, although it meant the loss of friends and left him on the foreign field, for the time being, without an appointment and without support; that Dr. A. T. Pierson, the able editor of the Missionary Review, asked baptism at the hands of Spurgeon's brother, when he knew such a course would put him out of favor with his beloved people, the Presbyterians; that G. Campbell Morgan, the spiritual teacher and prophet of God, felt impelled to immerse his own son who joined a Congregational Church; and Billy Sunday, marvelous combination of physical energy, youthful enthusiasm and passionate evangelism, was satisfied with nothing but immersion for himself. Our Saviour gave three commands which his disciples are to obey to the end of the world, viz., Make disciples, baptize and teach. Baptism stands between the two great experiences of regeneration (make disciples), and sanctification (teaching them to observe all things). Standing on this lofty position, baptism symbolizes the essential facts of Christianity in the past, present and future. That is, it embodies three fundamental ideas, (1) the fact of Christ's death and resurrection—historical Christianity; (2) the regeneration of the soul, buried with him by baptism and raised to walk in newness of life—living Christianity; (3) the final resurrection of the body—prophetic Christianity. Baptism is an epitome of Christ's message to the world: "More beautiful than figures of speech, more accurate than any statement of the lips, more complete than the articles of any creed." We show our love by obeying Christ implicitly. Abraham had the peculiar distinction of being called "the friend of God." Every believer may have the same distinction. "Ye are my

friends if ye do whatsoever I have commanded you." My Christian friends, have
you all been baptized? Not sprinkled or
poured, but baptized? If not, what will you
do with the positive command and plain example of Jesus, "Why call ye me Lord and
keep not my commandments?"

IV.

THE RECURRENT CHURCH ORDINANCE.

The record of the institution of the Lord's Supper is found in four places in the Bible. That we may have these Scriptures before us, I quote them. "And as they were eating, Jesus took bread, and blessed it, and brake it, and gave it to the disciples, and said, Take, eat; this is my body. And he took the cup, and gave thanks, and gave it to them, saying, Drink ye all of it; for this is my blood of the new testament, which is shed for many for the remission of sins." (Matt. 26:26-28.)

"For I have received of the Lord that which also I delivered unto you, that the Lord Jesus, the same night in which He was betrayed, took bread: And when he had given thanks, he brake it, and said, Take, eat; this is my body, which is broken for you; this do in remembrance of me. After the same manner also he took the cup, when he had supped, saying, This cup is the new testament in my blood: This do ye, as oft as ye drink it, in

remembrance of me.   For as often as ye eat
this bread, and drink this cup, ye do shew the
Lord's death till He come."   (1 Cor. 11:23-
26.)

"And he took bread, and gave thanks, and
brake it, and gave unto them saying, This is
my body which is given for you: this do in
remembrance of me.   Likewise also the cup
after supper, saying, This cup is the new
testament in my blood, which is shed for you."
(Luke 22:19, 20.)

"And as they did eat, Jesus took bread,
and blessed, and brake it, and gave to them,
and said, Take, eat; this is my body.   And
he took the cup, and when he had given
thanks, he gave it to them: and they all drank
of it.   And he said unto them, This is my
blood of the new testament, which is shed for
many."   (Mark 14:22-24.)

This is the second of two ordinances which
Christ gave to his church.   In the preceding
chapter we considered the first—baptism—
and saw that immersion was unquestionably
the practice in New Testament times, and
was the command of Jesus to every believer.
The world is coming back to New Testament

practice in its admission of immersion only as baptism, and Baptists have practically won their fight for the mode and meaning of this ordinance. The best scholarship of the world is with the Baptists. One of the handsomest new Episcopal churches in Virginia is provided with a pool. The rector is reported as saying: "The world is returning to the original mode of baptism."

We cannot say as much for our position regarding the Lord's Supper. That position is not so well understood as is our position on baptism, and there is an erroneous sentiment, in the minds of many, concerning the Lord's Supper, which makes it difficult to explain just what we believe about this ordinance, and our reasons for that belief.

The Baptist Position Stated.

The Christian world is divided into at least four divisions upon the Lord's Supper. The Catholics believe in transubstantiation, that is, the bread and wine are changed into the actual body and blood of Christ, and when you partake of these elements you do actually eat of the body and drink of the blood of

Christ.   This conversion of the elements into the flesh and blood of Christ is under the consecration of the priest.   The Lutherans and some others hold to what is called consubstantiation, that is, "the body and blood of Christ are truly present and are there communicated to those that eat in the Lord's Supper," but this presence is by virtue of Christ's word rather than the priest's consecration.   The Calvinists hold "that the body and blood are present in efficacy through the working of the Holy Spirit in the believing elect."   The Baptists believe that the bread is only a symbol of the body of Christ, and likewise the wine, of the blood.   We say there is no difference between this bread and other bread of the same kind except in the purpose for which it is used.   It is just bread and wine, that is all.   Against the Catholics, who say that the church, by a consecrating act, converts the elements into the body of Christ, and against the Lutherans, who say that the real body and blood are present because Christ said so, and against the Calvinists and all others who say there is a spiritual blessing and means of grace in the supper, we say, "No, the bread and wine only represent the flesh and blood," as where Christ in the parable of the sower said the seed is the word and the field is the world, he meant that the seed sown represent the word and the field where the seed were sown represents the world. We say there is no more efficacy in the Lord's Supper than in baptism. Each is a symbol and the only blessing is that which comes from obedience to Christ and from meditating upon the truths set forth in those symbols. So that, not to invite one to the Lord's Supper is not shutting him off from a means of grace. Those who take so much to heart the action of Baptists in not inviting them to the table, seem to think there is some mysterious grace in the supper just as they seem to think there is some efficacious power in the water of baptism. No, the baptism is only a picture setting forth Christ's burial and resurrection, and the supper is only a picture of Christ's death. By it we commemorate the sufferings and death of our Saviour and profess to be in communion with him. There is no hint of observing it in remembrance of one another,

nor for the expression of affection and fellowship.   Dr. Burrows, Sr., used to say, "Every
reference to the supper in the New Testament
connects it with Jesus."   To make either of
these ordinances mean more, is a perversion
of Scripture.   Every Baptist believes this
much about baptism, and if he is logical he
will believe the same about the Lord's Supper.

This is our position as to the import of the
Lord's Supper. Our practice has been severely
criticised by those who would have been milder
and more generous if they had understood our
interpretation of the meaning of the ordinance.
What is there objectionable in our practice?
Let me state that practice in one sentence—
We do not invite unbaptized persons to the
Lord's table, and as we do not extend invita-
tions to such persons, we do not accept in-
vitations of unbaptized persons to partake
with them.   Thinking as we do, that the
Lord's Supper is a church ordinance to be
preceded by baptism, we could not act otherwise.   And since the ordinance is not a means
of grace, we have not deprived those whom
we do not invite of any mysterious or special
blessing.   I candidly affirm that our posi-

tion is both scriptural and logical. And I say furthermore that while you may be a Baptist and be an open communionist, yet your brother who believes in restricted communion is more consistent than you.

The Baptist Position Vindicated.

We have seen that immersion was the uniform practice of Christ and his apostles. Having explained our belief and practice, it is now proposed to give a reason for our custom.

Proposition I.—There is no such thing in the Bible as free and open communion.

1. Restricted and located in the church. "For first of all, when ye come together in the church, I hear that there be divisions among you; and I partly believe it." 1 Cor. 11:18.

The ordinance is not to be observed in the home. Administering the supper in rooms of the sick and dying is not only contrary to Scripture teaching and practice as to the place for its observance, but is also to teach that there is some saving merit in the supper itself. Baptism of the dying comes from the same beliefs, namely, that the ordinance is essential to salvation. A more deadly or more anti-scriptural heresy never blighted a land.

2. Restricted to the pure in life. "But now I have written unto you not to keep company, if any man that is called a brother be a fornicator, or covetous, or an idolater, or a railer, or a drunkard, or an extortioner; with such an one no, not to eat." 1 Cor. 5:11.

3. Restricted to an orderly walk. "And now we command you, brethren, in the name of the Lord Jesus, that ye withdraw yourselves from every brother that walketh disorderly, and not after the tradition which he received of us." 2 Thess. 3:6.

The disorderly member is out of the church and hence away from the table. If I were a member of a Pedo-baptist church and should preach the doctrine I now hold, they would exclude me for heresy. Being excluded, they would not invite me to the table. But, holding these same views, and being a Baptist, they invite me to the table. That is, they are better to me as a Baptist than they would be if I belonged to them. This is inconsistent and unnatural.

4. Restricted to discernment of the Lord's body. "For he that eateth and drinketh unworthily, eateth and drinketh damnation to himself, not discerning the Lord's body." 1 Cor. 11:29.

One dare not think of wife or friends at the table of the Lord. Scripture, not sentiment, is the guide, and Paul says one must discriminate, must see, the Lord's body.

5. Restricted where divisions and schisms exist. 1 Cor. 11:17-20. Note the twentieth verse as it reads in the Revised Version, "When therefore ye assemble yourselves together, it is not possible to eat the Lord's Supper." The margin of the Authorized Version reads, "Ye cannot eat," and the reason assigned is the existence of divisions or schisms. Let us suppose the Catholics, Presbyterians, Methodists, Disciples, Episcopalians and Baptists assembled around one table to observe the Lord's Supper. Now, we have what the Christian world needs! The one thing supposed by many as wanting for the speedy conquest of the world for Christ is supplied! How beautiful to see all denominations around one table! But, wait a

moment before you break that bread. "Are
you agreed in other matters now that you
have come to a common table?" "Are you
united in doctrine and practice?" If there
be divisions among you there "you cannot
eat." The Catholic believes in an infallible
pope and a church through which alone people
are saved. The Presbyterian detests Roman
Catholicism, but believes that children of
believing parents are to be members of the
church. The Methodist believes in Ar-
minianism to an extent which separates him
widely from the Presbyterian. The Disciple
parts company with the sprinkling Methodist
and discards his emotional religion. The
Episcopalian declares his belief in Apostolic
succession and cannot accept Presbyterian,
Methodist, Disciple and Baptist pastors as
ordained ministers. The Baptist believes that
Jesus is the only Lord of the conscience and
that the New Testament is the only law of
Christianity. He tells the Catholic that his
claims are monstrous and preposterous; he
tells the Presbyterian that only believers
are to be members of the church; he tells the
Methodist that God is sovereign and His

purposes are behind and above all; he tells the Disciple, "With the heart man believeth," and not the head; he tells the Episcopalian that his church came from the Roman Catholics and his exclusive claim for an ordained ministry is a vestige of papal succession heresy and is absurd. Not to mention more, these are radical differences which exist among these denominations irrespective of the communion question. If they partake of that ordinance with these divisions among them, they do so as Paul says, "Not for the better but for the worse." Open communion would be an unmitigated curse.

6. Restricted to the baptized.

(1) Only the apostles were present at the institution. Neither his mother nor brothers were present, for they were unbaptized. We know that some of these twelve apostles were former disciples of John and he baptized all those whom he received. We know that Jesus himself was baptized, and can you believe that he used unbaptized persons as his apostles? The qualification of an apostle, as learned from the election of a successor to Judas, was that he should have companied

with Jesus and the eleven from the baptism
of John.

(2) *The supper comes after baptism.*

The divine order is, (1) disciple; (2) baptize; (3) teach all the things commanded.
The order is a part of that commission. You
have as much right to put baptism before
making disciples as you have to put communion before baptism.   Dr. Hibbard, Methodist, truly writes: "The reader will perceive
that the argument is based entirely upon the
order of the apostolic commission. It may
be questioned by some whether the argument
is genuine, and whether it is entitled to any
considerable force. But suppose we assume
an opposite ground? Suppose we say that
the things commanded are important to be
done, but the order observed in the commission is a subject of indifference. Now what
will be the consequences of this position?
What but total, irretrievable confusion? The
apostles go forth, they are intent upon doing
all that Christ commanded them, but the
order of the duties is a subject of indifference.
The consequence is that some are baptized
before they are converted from heathenism;

some receive the holy supper before either baptism or conversion; others are engaged in a course of instruction before they are discipled; and the most incoherent and unsuitable practices everywhere prevail. Improper persons are baptized, or baptism is improperly delayed; the holy supper is approached before the candidate is duly prepared, and it is therefore desecrated, or it is unduly withheld from rightful communicants. Is not the prescribed order therefore in the administration of the ordinances, and the duties of the apostolic commission all-important? And thus we hold that Christ enjoined the order as well as the duties themselves; and, in this order of Christ, baptism precedes communion at the Lord's table."

(3) The practice of the Apostles.

The first instance of the Lord's Supper being observed after its institution. "Then they that gladly received his word were baptized and the same day there were added unto them about three thousand souls. And they continued steadfastly in the apostles' doctrine and fellowship, and in breaking of bread, and in prayers." Acts 2:41, 42.

The second instance of the Lord's Supper after its institution. "And upon the first day of the week, when the disciples came together to break bread, Paul preached unto them, ready to depart on the morrow; and continued his speech until midnight." Acts 20:7.

(4) Every mention of baptism puts it immediately upon profession of faith and hence before the Lord's Supper.

The Samaritans believed Philip and were baptized at once. Acts 8:12. The Eunuch believed Philip and was baptized immediately. Acts 8:36-39. Paul was baptized as soon as the scales fell from his eyes. Acts 9:18. The jailer was baptized the same hour of the night. Acts 16:33.

There is not a case in which there was time to celebrate the Lord's Supper before baptism. If we do not know from the New Testament that immersion was their baptism, then we do not know from the Bible that there is a God. If we do not know from the same source that immersion came before the supper, then we do not know that there were any believers or churches. I assert in the words of Dr. Jeter, "In all the oracles of God there is neither proof that the Lord's Supper was ever administered but within a church and to its baptized members." In what chapter and verse do you find your authority for an unbaptized person partaking of the Lord's Supper? Do you believe that immersion only is baptism? Then you must be a restricted communionist, for you cannot show where an unbaptized person ever partook of the supper in the New Testament.

(5) That we are right in demanding baptism as a prerequisite to the supper is evident from the symbolism of the ordinances. Baptism symbolizes spiritual birth. Birth precedes nourishment. The Lord's Supper symbolizes spiritual nourishment, support. We are born once and baptized once. We are fed often, and have the Lord's Supper often.

Proposition II.—There is no such thing among the denominations as open and free communion.

The Rev. Dr. William Wall, of the Church of England, who wrote two large and elaborate volumes of the history of infant baptism, showing that immersion was uniformly practiced in the early churches, says: "No church ever gave the communion to any person before he was baptized; among all absurdities ever held, none ever held this, that any person should partake of the communion before he was baptized."

Among the Presbyterians, the devout and erudite Dr. Doddridge writes: "It is certain that so far as our knowledge of primitive antiquity extends, no unbaptized person received the Lord's Supper. Howsoever excellent any man's character is, he must be baptized before he can be looked upon as completely a member of the church of Christ."

Rev. Dr. Griffin, one of the most eminent Congregational divines of this country, writes: "I agree with the advocates of close communion * * * that we ought not to commune with those who have not been baptized, and of course are not church members, even if we regard them as Christians."

Among the Methodist scholars and divines, Rev. Dr. Hibbard writes: "It is but just to remark that in one principle the Baptist and Pedo-baptist churches agree. They both agree in rejecting from the table of the Lord and in denying the rights of church fellowship to all who have not been baptized. Valid baptism they (Baptists) consider essential to constitute visible church membership. This we (Methodists) also hold. The only question, then, that divides us is, What is valid baptism? No society of Christians would receive an unbaptized person into its community and tender to him the privileges of their body * * * The converts of the day of Pentecost were first baptized, and then added to the church. The concurrent voice of the Christian world would exclude an unbaptized person from fellowship in the visible church of Christ."

The Episcopalians declare that baptism and church membership precede communion. Prof. Cheetham, Professor of Pastoral Theology in King's College, London, says: "None could be admitted to holy communion but baptized persons lying under no censure."

The Episcopal Recorder says: "The close communion of the Baptist churches is but the necessary sequence of the fundamental idea out of which their existence has grown. No Christian church would willingly receive to its communion even the humblest and truest believer in Christ who had not been baptized. With Baptists immersion only is baptism, and they therefore, of necessity, exclude from the Lord's table all who have not been immersed. It is an essential part of the system—the legitimate carrying out of the creed."

Lord Chancellor King says: "As for the persons communicating, they were not indifferently all that professed the Christian faith, as Origen writes: 'It doth not belong to every one to eat of the bread, and to drink of this cup.' But they were only such as were in the number of the faithful, 'such as were baptized, and received both the credentials and practices of Christianity.' That is, who believe the articles of the Christian faith and led a holy and pious life. Such as these, and none else, were permitted to communicate. Now since none but the faithful were admitted, it follows that the catechumens and the penitents were excluded; the catechumens because they were not yet baptized, for baptism always precedes the Lord's Supper."

Therefore Dr. Cuyler says: "The terms of communion in the Presbyterian Church require a previous open confession of the Lord Jesus Christ as Saviour and Lord. That presupposes a membership in some evangelical church. Baptism is an essential part of an open profession of Jesus Christ and of reception into the visible church."

John Wesley says very plainly that baptism precedes communion. In a sermon which he preached upon "Do this in remembrance of me," he laid down baptism as a prerequisite to communion. (Wesley's Sermons, vol. 4, p. 153.) In his Journal, vol. 1, p. 188, he says: "In the ancient times every one who was baptized communicated daily." No Baptist ever insisted upon this doctrine more strongly than did Mr. Wesley.

In practice Mr. Wesley was as strict as any high-churchman in the land. Commenting upon a letter received from one J. M. Bolzins, he says: "And yet this very man, when I was in Savannah, did I refuse to admit to the Lord's table, because he was not baptized by a minister who had been episcopally ordained."

In reply to a question from Mr. Jones, of England, Mr. Alexander Campbell says:

"Your third question is, Do any of your churches admit unbaptized persons to communion, a practice that is becoming very prevalent in this country? Not one so far as is known to me. I am at loss to understand on what principle—by what law, precedent or license any congregation founded upon the apostles and prophets, Jesus Christ being the chief corner stone, could dispense with the practice of the primitive church with the commandment of the Lord and the authority of the apostles."

In the Christian Baptist Mr. Campbell says: "But I object to making it a rule, in any case, to receive unimmersed persons to church ordinances: first, because it is nowhere commanded; second, because it is nowhere precedented in the New Testament; third, because it necessarily corrupts the simplicity and uniformity of the whole genius of the New Testament; fourth, because it not only deranges the order of the kingdom, but makes void one of the most important institutions ever given to men."

Then, if there is no such thing in the Bible or among the denominations as open communion, why blame the Baptists for consistency and conscientiousness? The average Pedo-baptist to-day disregards the standard authorities of his denomination and views the Lord's Supper sentimentally. He ignores the logic of restricted communion and conceives it as a breach of Christian fellowship, a denial of a common faith. He does not distinguish between Christian and church fellowship. He fails to see the logic of his own position. Sentiment is not a safe criterion; it is as variable as a weather vane. The Scriptures are the one unerring, unchangeable guide. Adherence to their teachings is obligatory. The very essence of the Lord's Supper is changed when sentiment controls its observance. Suppose the sentiment of missionaries in China favored admission of cultured Confucianists to the Lord's Table as a recognition of their moral code. The perception of Christ's broken body would be lost thereby for sentimental reasons. Yet the logic that abolishes the prerequisite of baptism would, strictly applied, lead to the abolition of the symbolism of the elements, leaving the ordinance like a monument whose inscription had been effaced, like a temple whose glory had departed.

Objections Removed.

1. A Baptist wife cannot commune with her Pedo-baptist husband or vice versa. This objection is based upon an erroneous view of the purpose of the Lord's Supper. "The cup of blessing which we bless, is it not a participation of the blood of Christ? The bread which we break, is it not a participation of the body of Christ?" 1 Cor. 10:17. It is communion with Christ and never communion with friends or loved ones. You commune with them in your homes. A husband and wife are to show their love for each other in the home, and day by day.

2. If we cannot partake of the communion together on earth, how can we in heaven? This question would never be asked by one who has noted the time limit on the Lord's Supper. There will be no Lord's Supper in heaven. Christ said it was to be kept "until he come."

3. The Baptists are a narrow folk because they do not commune with other denomina-

tions. We do commune with them in every legitimate way. We commune with them in gospel song, in earnest prayers, in enterprises of benevolence, in temperance reform and in moral welfare. Baptists contribute to hospitals and charitable objects like other people. They are just as liberal with their means and in their views as other people. I am sure they are not less hospitable. Baptists invite all denominations to their tables and make no distinction in dispensing the hospitality of their homes. They invite all to *their* tables, but to the *Lord's* table they can invite only those whom he has invited, that is, baptized persons.

4. Restricted communion prevents Christian union. Why do not the denominations that believe in open communion unite as they are? When they have done so then it will be time to make this objection to the Baptists. I venture that the Methodists and Presbyterians are as far apart as they would be if the Baptists were open communionists.

5. Restricted communion keeps many out of the Baptist denomination. So does our

requirement of a changed life. We could not surrender a principle to increase our membership. Furthermore, when those who incline towards the Baptists understand why restricted communion is practiced they will be drawn to us more readily and closely. Even outsiders who understand our position admire and commend us for our consistency. We are always glad to have accessions, but we are also anxious that they shall be right in belief and practice. Then, again, it does not seem that restricted communion is hurting us badly, for in the South, where Baptists are uniformly restricted communionists, they are growing faster than anywhere else in the world. God honors the people who honor His word. We have no desire for a liberality that breaks a Bible commandment or changes a gospel order. We are content to be as broad as Jesus Christ.

It is submitted that Baptists are not responsible for existing divisions. Baptists have adhered to a uniform scriptural practice. The people who deviated from the course of the New Testament are responsible for the divisions.

V.

WHAT OTHERS SAY ABOUT THEM.

When one reflects upon the assurance with which informed and loyal Baptists hold their tenets to be scriptural, the wonder arises how so many devout Christians justify themselves in not subscribing to Baptist views. Upon investigation, using only books immediately at hand by *non-Baptists*, it is highly gratifying to find the substantiation of our doctrines by numerous historians and commentators. This increases surprise at the position of our Pedo-baptist friends. Their own writers, by direct statement or implication, admit much for which Baptists contend. Non-Christian authorities are equally explicit. Reference to other libraries than my own would have increased the number of authorities indefinitely. By using second-hand data the task could have been performed quickly. Ignoring all quotations from books by Baptist authors, or quotations of Pedo-baptists by Baptists, this independent investigation was made. The results, not to repeat matter used elsewhere in this book, follow.

Views of Three Encyclopedias.

1. American Encyclopedia Britannica.

"The Baptists were the first denomination of British Christians that undertook the work of missions to the heathen, which has become so prominent a feature in the religious activity of the present century. As early as the year 1784, the Northamptonshire Association of Baptist Churches resolved to recommend that the first Monday of every month should be set apart for prayer for the spread of the gospel, a practice which has since, as a German writer remarks, extended over all Protestant Christendom, and we may add over all Protestant Missions." Vol. II, page 796.

2. The Jewish Encyclopedia.

"A Christian denomination or sect denying the validity of infant baptism or of any baptism not preceded by a profession of faith. Baptists and their spiritual progenitors, the Anabaptists of the sixteenth century (including the Mennonites), have always made liberty of conscience a cardinal doctrine.

Balthasar Hubmaier, the Anabaptist leader, in his tract on "Heretics and Their Burners" (1524), insisted that not only heretical Christians, but also Turks and Jews were to be won to the truth by moral suasion alone, not by fire or sword; yet as a Catholic, but a few years before, he had co-operated in the destruction of a Jewish synagogue in Regensburg and in the expulsion of the Jews from the city. * * * The Mennonites of the Netherlands, who became wealthy during the seventeenth century, were so broad-minded and philanthropic that they made large contributions for the relief of persecuted Jews. In England, Henry Jessey, one of the most learned of the Baptist ministers of the middle decades of the seventeenth century (1649 onward), was an enthusiastic student of Hebrew and Aramaic, and an ardent friend of the oppressed Hebrews of his time." Vol. II, page 501. This article, written by Newman, has the imprimatur of the Hebrew editors.

3. The Catholic Encyclopedia.

"The Baptists consider the Scriptures to be the sufficient and exclusive rule of faith and practice. In the interpretation of them every individual enjoys restricted freedom. No non-scriptural scheme of doctrine and duty is recognized as authoritative. General creeds are mere declarations of prevalent doctrinal views, to which no assent beyond one's personal conviction need be given. * * * Baptists hold that those only are members of the Church of Christ who have been baptized upon making a personal profession of faith. They agree in the rejection of infant baptism as contrary to the Scriptures, and in the acceptance of immersion as the sole valid mode of baptism. All children who die before the age of responsibility will nevertheless be saved. Baptism and the Eucharist, the only two sacraments, or ordinances as they call them, which Baptists generally admit, are not productive of grace, but are mere symbols. Baptism does not bestow, but symbolizes, regeneration, which has already taken place. In the Eucharist Jesus Christ is not really present; the Lord's Supper merely sets forth the death of Christ as the sustaining power of the believer's life. It was instituted for the followers of Christ alone; hence Baptists, in theory, commonly admit to it only their own church members and exclude outsiders (close communion). Open communion, however, has been practiced extensively in England and is gaining ground to-day among American Baptists. In church polity, the Baptists are congregational, i. e., each church enjoys absolute automony. Its only officers are the elders or bishops and the deacons. The elder exercises the different pastoral functions and the deacon is his assistant in both spiritual and temporal concerns. These officers are chosen by common suffrage and ordained by "Councils" consisting of ministers and representatives of neighboring churches. A church may, in case of need, appeal for help to another church; it may, in difficulty, consult other churches; but never, even in such cases, can members of one congregation acquire authority over another congregation. Much less can a secular power interfere in spiritual affairs. Vol. II., page 278.

The Initial Ordinance.

1. Cunningham Geikie, Episcopalian: "John resisted no longer, and leading Jesus into the stream, the rite was performed * * *

Holy and pure before sinking under the waters, he must yet have risen from them with the light of a higher glory in his countenance." "Life and Words of Christ," pages 413 and 414.

2. Neander, converted Jew: "In respect to the form of baptism, it was in conformity with the original institution and the original import of the symbol, performed by immersion. * * * Baptism was administered at first only to adults, as men were accustomed to conceive baptism and faith as strictly connected. We have all reason for not deriving infant baptism from apostolic institution, and the recognition of it which followed somewhat later, as an apostolical tradition, serves to confirm this hypothesis. "History of the Christian Religion and Church." Vol. I., pages 310 and 311.

3. G. Campbell Morgan, immersed Congregationalist: "He (Jesus) left the seclusion and the privacy, and standing on the threshold of public work, with the waters of a death baptism, which he had shared in the grace of his heart with man, still clinging about him, the silent heavens broke into the lan-

guage of a great music, as the Almighty Father declared, 'This is My beloved Son, in whom I am well pleased.' " "The Crisis of the Christ," page 136.

4. Dr. Phillip Schaff, Presbyterian: In the encyclopedia of which he was co-editor, he secured Dr. Osgood to write the article on Baptism (The Baptist View). He follows that with a lengthy discussion by himself. Though differing from the "Baptist View," his scholarship compelled him to say, "There is no trace of infant baptism in the New Testament. All attempts to deduce it from the words of institution, or from such passages as 1 Cor. 1:16, must be given up as arbitrary." "Baptism in the early church was a triple immersion." "The Council of Ravenna (1311) was the first to allow a choice between sprinkling and immersion." Vol. I., page 200-ff.

"Augustine, Gregory Nazianzen and Chrysostom had Christian mothers, but were not baptized till they were converted in early manhood." Schaff-Herzog Encyclopedia of Religious Knowledge. Vol. I., page 210.

Dean Stanley, Episcopalian: In a graphic

description of baptism in the patristic age, says, "They then plunged into the water. Both before and after the immersion," etc. "Christian Institutions," page 5.

5. H. M. Gwatkin, Presbyterian: "We have good evidence that infant baptism is no direct institution either of the Lord himself or of his apostles. There is no trace of it in the New Testament. Every discussion of this subject presumes persons old enough to have faith and repentance, and no case of baptism is recorded except of such persons, for the whole 'household' mentioned would in that age mean dependents and slaves as naturally as they suggest children to the English reader." "Early Christian History, A. D. 313." Vol. I., page 251.

6. John Wesley, Methodist: He was indicted by a grand jury at Savannah August, 1737, upon ten counts; the fifth arraignment was that he had broken the laws of the realm by "refusing to baptize Mr. Parker's child, *other than by dipping*, except the parents would certify it was weak, and not able to bear it." "The Heart of Wesley's Journal," page 21.

7. Dr. William Sanday, Episcopalian: "Baptism has a double function: (1) It brings the Christian into personal contact with Christ so close that it may be fitly described as union with him; (2) it expresses symbolically a series of acts corresponding to the redeeming acts of Christ.

Immersion—Death.

Submersion — Burial (the ratification of death).

Emergence—Resurrection.

All these the Christian has to undergo in a moral and spiritual sense, and by means of his union with Christ." "The International Critical Commentary on Romans," page 153.

8. Jas. Cardinal Gibbons, Roman Catholic: "For several centuries after the establishment of Christianity baptism was *usually* conferred by immersion; but since the twelfth century the practice of baptizing by infusion has prevailed in the Catholic Church, as this manner is attended with less inconvenience than baptism by immersion." This paragraph occurs, to be sure, in an argument for baptismal regeneration and for the discretion of "the Church" in adopting the most convenient

mode; but it is striking that the distinguished Cardinal felt constrained to concede so much to immersion. ("The Faith of Our Fathers," page 277, eighty-third edition.)

Church Officers.

1. The noted skeptic and historian Gibbon: "The primitive bishops were considered only as the first of their equals, and the honorable servants of a free people. Whenever the episcopal chair became vacant by death, a new president was chosen among the presbyters by the suffrage of the whole congregation, every member of which supposed himself invested with a sacred and sacerdotal character. Such was the mild and equal constitution by which the Christians were governed more than a hundred years after the death of the apostles. Every society formed itself within a separate and independent republic; and although the most distant of these little States maintained a mutual as well as friendly intercourse of letters and deputations, the Christian world was not yet connected by any supreme authority or legis-

lative assembly." "Roman Empire," vol.
I., page 413.

2. Professor Kurtz, Lutheran: "It is un-
equivocably testified by the New Testament,
and, as appears from the First Epistle of
Clement of Rome (ch. 42, 44, 57), the fact
had never been disputed down to the close of
the first century, that bishops and presbyters
are identical. The force of this objection,
however, is sought to be obviated by the
subterfuge that while all bishops were indeed
presbyters, all presbyters were not bishops.
The ineptitude of such an evasion is apparent.
In Phil. 1:1, the apostle, referring to this one
particular church, greeted not one but several
bishops. According to Acts 20:17, 28, all
the presbyters of the one Ephesian church are
made bishops by the Holy Ghost. Also
Titus 1:5, 7 unconditionally excludes such a
distinction; and according to 1 Peter 5:2 all
such presbyters should be *episkopountes*. In
opposition to this theory, which received
the sanction of the Council of Trent, the old
Protestant theologians maintained the original
identity of the two names and offices. In
support of this they could refer not only to

the New Testament, but also to Clement of Rome and the Teaching of the Twelve Apostles, where, just as in Phil. 1:1, only bishops and deacons are named as church officers, and as appointed by the free choice of the church. They can also point to the consensus of the most respected church fathers and church teachers of the later times." "Church History," pages 54 and 59.

3. H. M. Gwatkins, Presbyterian: "That the 'bishops' in the New Testament were not what we call bishops is proved at once by the single fact that there were sundry of them at Philippi. They evidently stand in close relation to the elders. Thus the elders of Ephesus are reminded that they are bishops, and the qualifications of the bishops and elders as described to Timothy and Titus are nearly the same, and point to oversight certainly, and to the same sort of oversight, but to oversight which is pastoral, not what we should call episcopal. Again, St. Paul's argument from the bishop to the elder would be no argument at all if the bishops were already no more than a small class among the elders. The rough general equivalence of

bishops and elders in the New Testament
has very seldom been disputed since the controversies of the seventeenth century. * * *
We find no trace of bishops in the New Testament." "Early Church History to A. D.
313," vol. I., pages 69 and 72.

Church Government.

1. Viscount Bryce, Episcopalian, tracing
the rise of the hierarchy, draws an analogy
from the growth of the empire and gives a
passing notice to the freedom of the earliest
churches. "And, just as with the extension
of the empire all the independent rights of
districts, towns, or tribes had disappeared, so
now the primitive freedom and diversity of
individual Christians and local churches, already circumscribed by the frequent struggles
against heresy, was finally overborne by the
idea of one visible catholic church, uniform in
faith and ritual." "Holy Roman Empire,"
page 30.

2. Jefferson, Unitarian, may not have gotten
his scheme for our government from a Baptist
Church, but he wrote a fine definition of
church government. "Each church being

free, no one can have jurisdiction over another one." "I cannot give up my guidance to the magistrate, because he knows no more the way to heaven than I do, and is less concerned to direct me right than I am to go." "The Writings of Thomas Jefferson." Library Edition, Vol. XVII, 9.

3. Professor Kurtz, in his monumental work, shows the equality of believers in the churches: "As in those Hellenic associations all ranks, even those which in civil society were separated from one another by impassable barriers, found admission, and then, in the framing of statutes, the reception of fellow members, the exercise of discipline, possessed equal rights." "Church History," page 54.

4. A Congregationalist author, in a recent illuminating book, when discussing the early churches in the Roman Empire, says: "These churches, for many years, were little independent democracies, with no special distinctions between laity and clergy; there were no real *clerical orders* for a long time. Their officers were elective, and subject to removal by popular vote. The various churches were

bound together by brotherly feelings, but no
coercion was exercised by one church over
others." "The Winning of Religious Liberty,"
by Joseph H. Crooker, page 18.

Religious Liberty.

1. Thomas Jefferson, to his neighbors, the
members of the Baptist Church of Buck
Mountain, in Albemarle, April 13, 1809: "We
have acted together from the origin to the end
of a memorable revolution, and we have contributed, each in the line alloted us, our en-
deavors to render its issue a permanent blessing to our country. That our social intercourse may, to the evening of our days, be
cheered and cemented by witnessing the freedom and happiness for which we have labored,
will be my constant prayer. Accept the offering of my affectionate esteem and respect."
He wrote five letters to Baptist churches and
Associations.

2. George P. Fisher, Professor at Yale:
"A Baptist committee laid their complaints
before the Massachusetts delegates in the
first Continental Congress at Philadelphia.
The support which the Baptist lent to the

patriotic cause, and the proclamation of human rights which was made on every hand won a hearing for their demands and rendered them, after tedious delays, successful. In Virginia Patrick Henry, Jefferson and Madison enlisted in their favor. In 1785 the statute of religious freedom was adopted, of which Jefferson deemed it a great honor to have been the author, by which intervention in matters of faith and worship was forbidden to the State. All denominations were thus put on a level, and none were taxed for the support of religion." "History of the Christian Church," page 560.

3. Parton, after mentioning the address from the Baptists to the Virginia Convention, August 16, 1775, petitioning that four Baptist ministers should be allowed to preach to Baptist soldiers, cites the Convention's resolution which both granted the request and conceded the principle: "*Resolved*, That it be an instruction to the commanding officers of regiments or troops to be raised that they permit dissenting clergymen to celebrate divine worship, and to preach to the soldiers, or exhort, from time to time, as the various

operations of the military service may permit, for the ease of such scrupulous consciences as may not choose to attend divine worship as celebrated by the chaplain." He then adds a striking sentence: "Thus began religious equality in Virginia." "Life of Thomas Jefferson," by Parton, page 174.

4. Leonard Woolsey Bacon, Congregationalist: Discussing the establishment of the American principle of the non-interference of the State with religion and the equality of all religious communions before the law, concludes: "So far as this work was a work of intelligent conviction and religious faith, the chief honor of it must be given to the Baptists. Other sects, notably the Presbyterians, had been energetic and efficient in demanding their own liberties; the Friends and the Baptists agreed in demanding liberty of conscience and worship, and equality before the law, for all alike. But the active labor in this cause was mainly done by the Baptists. It is to their consistency and constancy in the warfare against the privileges of the powerful 'Standing Order' of New England, and of the moribund establishments of the South that

we are chiefly indebted for the final triumph in this country of that principle of the separation of Church and State which is one of the largest contributions of the New World to civilization and to the church universal." "A History of American Christianity," page 221.

5. "In England, from the time of Henry VIII to William III, a full century and a half, the Baptists struggled to gain their footing and to secure liberty of conscience for all. From 1611 they issued appeal after appeal, addressed to the King, the Parliament, and the people, in behalf of 'soul liberty,' written with a breadth of view and force of argument hardly since exceeded. Yet, until the Quakers arose in 1660, the Baptists stood alone in its defense, amid universal opposition * * * Among the Baptists Christian freedom found its earliest, its staunchest, its most consistent, and its most disinterested champion. * * * Not less powerful has been the influence of the Baptists in the United States. * * * Persecuted themselves, they never persecuted others. * * * The paths of the Baptists

are paths of freedom, pleasantness and peace."
(Appleton's American Encyclopedia, Vol. II,
page 293-f.)

Conclusion.

Joseph H. Crooker, Congregationalist: "The
Baptists are the least sacramental and the
most scriptural of the Protestant denominations." "Winning of Religious Liberty," page
204.

VI.

STATE AND CHURCH: A PRESENT PROBLEM.

We have been passing through unusual times. The war has changed many things—some for better and some for worse. The government has insisted upon the subordination of everything else to one object, "the winning of the war." Right loyally have the people complied. They have surrendered their individual rights, sacrificed their own interests, and suppressed their own convictions in order that the government might have a free hand in carrying out its program. Where our people could not commend, they have kept silent. All this is indubitable proof of their patriotism. It is a refutation of the charge that democracy cannot co-ordinate and concentrate for a huge task.

Such submission to governmental authorities in time of war, however, does not signify that we have ceased to think for ourselves; nor is it to be interpreted as indicating that we have forgotten our religious rights and privileges in the American system; nor does it mean that we have permanently foregone the guaranteed right of free speech. If we have submitted where protest was unavailing, it was only for the time being. Now that the war is practically over, we may, with propriety, and must, in justice to our conscience, give expression to our convictions.

In general it may be said that the government in a military situation enters into a field in which it has no concern in normal civil life, namely, that of religion. Entering this field to meet a national emergency, the obligation is imperative to deal with all religious organizations in a spirit of scrupulous equity. To practice or allow any discrimination in such case is just as much a violation of the principles of religious liberty as if the government were to attempt in civil life to regulate the religious life of the people.

The government violated the priceless principle of "equal rights to all and special privileges to none" by admitting Roman Catholic organizations into the camps and excluding Episcopalians, Baptists, *et al*. The ground

for this action, we have heard, was that the
Y. M. C. A. represented the Protestant denominations, though accredited denominational representatives were not consulted in
the adoption of the plan.   It ignored the fact,
however, that to a Baptist his message is just
as precious and vital as the creed of the Roman
Catholic is to the Catholic.   It permitted the
denomination which stands for the authority
of the "church" to have access to the soldiers,
and denied that right to the denomination
which stands for the authority of the Bible.
It discriminated in favor of the Roman Catholics and against the Baptists and others.   As
an Episcopalian bishop recently said in my
hearing, having his own denomination in
mind: "The church should have the right to
follow her children.   The government called
our children into the service and then said to
the spiritual mother, 'You cannot follow and
minister to them as a church.' "   That, I
say respectfully, was going beyond the government's real authority and violating the principle laid down in the Bill of Rights and incorporated in the Constitution of the United
States.   It was a reversal of the policy of the

government which permitted voluntary preaching to soldiers in the Revolutionary and Confederate Wars.

Another instance of governmental meddling in religious and discrimination in favor of the Catholics was the order to merge the war service funds. If the Catholics were to be recognized as sufficiently separate and distinct and apart from others to be given special privileges in the camps, why should they be united with others when a campaign was to be made for funds? Had the Baptists been permitted to have their buildings in the camps they would have erected them and maintained them and would have provided the funds without asking the government or anybody else to aid them. The government gave access to the Catholics and denied it to the Baptists, and then violated its own rule, on which it admitted the Catholics, by lumping them with other war work activities when money was needed. Those who read know that this was not the original program, but that it was brought about after the Knights of Columbus held a meeting, in which they protested to the government and in some way in-

fluenced the President to change his mind and
merge the funds. Why is it that Catholic
protests are effective at the White House and
Baptist protests are not? If the Baptists
were not a people seven millions strong, if
they were only one million or one thousand
strong, that would not invalidate their rights
under the Constitution. Fair treatment
should be given to every denomination, irrespective of its size. It is antagonistic to the
very principle of separation of Church and
State for any church, particularly the one
which constantly meddles in State affairs,
to be given preference by civil authorities.
Baptists ask no special favors of the government; they ask only their inherent rights,
their constitutional privileges, and they will
be satisfied with nothing else.

Gladstone once said that it was the duty
of the government "to make it easy for people
to do right." The government made it hard
for Baptists to do their duty by the moral welfare of the men in the service, when it not
merely approved, but practically originated
and forced a joint campaign, by which Baptists had to give to Roman Catholic propa-

ganda, or be misjudged by their fellow citizens as penurious, bigoted and unpatriotic. It is not the point to say that the United War Work Campaign was a success. The machinery employed in that campaign and the patriotic temper of our people would make anything a success. Success does not validate wrong or injustice. The Catholics should have made the effort alone in raising funds for their special work, since they had sought and secured recognition by the government as being distinct from all others. The truth is, their failure to secure the amount sought in their first campaign made them apprehensive lest they should fail in a second. They used the opportunity in the united campaign to exploit their exaggerated numbers and proclaim their patriotism. They were the only ones in the joint meetings, so far as I heard, who had the poor taste to parade statistics and advertise the loyalty of their "church" in America. If some of us counted as they do, we would astound ourselves and others with startling statistics.

There is no need to say that the Catholic organization in the camps was not a propa ganda. We know better. If it were not a propaganda, how did it come about that in one camp in the South a priest proselyted eighty-odd Protestant young men; that in another camp a priest strung beads around a dying Protestant in the hospital and received him into the Roman Catholic Church before he died; that numbers of our young men whose eyes were open and who were alert to the insidious methods of Romanists have said personally or in letters that the Catholics were working for their ends, and that outsiders did not realize what they were doing; that Romanist services in the camps were featured and a press publicity given to them out of proportion to their importance and sometimes to the disparagement and neglect of Protestant services? The government might have known, from the whole history of the Romanists, what they would do under the special rights granted them in the camps. Professing to discountenance sectarianism in the army, the government made the egregious blunder of admitting to special privileges the most sectarian of the sects. The Romanists could not be true to their religion without propaganda and proselytism. They think that all outside of their church are lost, whether they be Presbyterians, Methodists, or what not, and they are conscientiously bound to put forth every effort to bring all others into their church.

Last of all came the proposal for a "Liberty Church" in the "Ordnance Reservations." These reservations are owned, or controlled, by the government for the making of explosives. The government admitted the Roman Catholics and the Jews to these reservations and said to all the other denominations, "You cannot come in except through the 'Liberty Church.'" "Liberty" is a misnomer. The rules for governing that "Church" show that it represents anything but "liberty." It is so regulated and restricted that the constituent members do not control. It is also an attempt at amalgamation, and, as Bishop Thompson said in a conference at Newport News, there is danger of "chemical reaction."

The government said bluntly that it is "impossible" to admit the denominations to these reservations. Why impossible? Take Penniman, for example—an ordnance reserva-

tion six miles from Williamsburg, Virginia.
One-half of the eight thousand people at
Penniman were Baptists, or from Baptist
families, or of Baptist inclination. They
said so by cards which they signed in the religious census of Penniman. Yet the Roman
Catholics, who represented only a small per
cent., were allowed to function at Penniman, and the Baptists, who represented fully
half of the people, were forbidden. The
government urged people to move to these
reservations and work on munitions. Baptists responded and took their wives and children and set up family life in the reservation,
and the government prescribed that they
should not have a church. Where is the
common sense, or the law, or the justice in
this? The government proposes to use certain of these plants as industrial reservations
and perpetuate the injustice to Baptists
that it perpetrated in time of war.

The promoter of the "Liberty Church," a
very amiable and earnest gentleman, by the
way, said, perhaps inadvertently, in the Newport News conference, that it was hoped that
when the war was over there would come

about from these "Liberty Churches" an interchange of church membership and open communion. The Baptist State Mission Board of Virginia sent a committee to the conference on the "Liberty Church," instructed to present the following resolutions:

1. We are earnestly desirous of co-operating in every possible way in caring for the religious life of the people in and round the ordnance reservations.

2. We consider the proposed plan of the "Liberty Church" undesirable and impracticable.

3. In our judgment, if the denominations are not to be permitted to function separately in the reservations, the object aimed at can be better attained by and through the Y. M. C. A.

4. We are ready to secure and contribute a fair percentage of such funds as may be necessary to support a Y. M. C. A. in each ordnance reservation.

It developed that the Episcopalians were almost as averse to the "Liberty Church" as were the Baptists. A bishop referred to the government's infringement upon religious freedom for which they had fought and, turning to a Baptist, he said, "and the Baptists also." We were glad to know that the Episcopalians were jealous for religious freedom and that they interpreted the proposal of the "Liberty Church" much as we did. It should make no headway. Why cannot the government see that it is best for the government and for the denominations and for all the people, to leave them free in the exercise of their religion? We shall prosper most under such a government. The denominations could function in a reservation of ten thousand people with as little friction as they do in a town of ten thousand people. If the government could only realize that it is not competent to manage the religion of the people it would escape many a blunder.

More than ever is one convinced of the wisdom of the Baptist position and the necessity for presenting our views clearly and forcefully and fraternally. As we once took the lead in winning and establishing religious freedom we should now take the lead in clarifying and preserving it. We might waive the declarations of our Baptist people under the old regime of religious oppression; we might leave others to narrate our struggles for entire separation of Church and State and confine the issue to just one question: "Shall the government abide by the will of the people as incorporated in the laws of the States and Nation?" On that issue we would submit that all the Bills of Rights provide for full freedom of religious opinion and worship, and for equality before the law of all religious denominations and their members; and many forbid the establishment of any particular church or sect, and declare that no public money ought to be applied in aid of any religious body or sectarian institution.

Furthermore, we would submit that the Constitution specifies that "Congress shall make no law respecting an establishment of religion, or prohibiting the free exercise thereof." Congress is the only law-making body, and what it cannot do an official or department or board or an agent of the government cannot do. And what cannot be done directly cannot be done indirectly. Yet, when four thousand Baptist people in an industrial reservation are told they cannot have a Baptist Church where they are asked by the government to live and work, and when seven million Baptists are forbidden to minister to their members in the camps, it is both an evasion and a violation of the fundamental law of the land, by officials who have no constitutional prerogatives in the matter. When the government offers to build a church on government land for Roman Catholics it is appropriating public funds for sectarian purposes. When it forbids the Baptists to erect a building at their own expense in such a reservation it is destroying "the equality before the law of all religious denominations." A sentence from "Notes on Virginia" is as true now as it was in 1781: "It is error alone which needs the support of government. Truth can stand by itself." It appears that some of the "powers that be" care nothing "for full freedom of religious opinion and worship." I am aware that religious freedom is a civil right, and that in times of war necessities and emergencies may alter, for the time being, this right; but I am not aware of any authority in war or in peace for inequality, unfairness, and injustice towards any denomination or for governmental assumption of religious functions.

VII.

THEIR POSITION IN THE TWENTIETH CENTURY.

Baptists are like the immortal marines—everyone is a volunteer. There is not a conscript among them. They should be more strongly bound together than any other religious group, because each one entered its bonds of his own accord. Common convictions cement them. They believe, therefore they speak and act. They are rooted and grounded in the New Testament.

Their *origin is scriptural.* The first Baptist churches were the churches of the New Testament. It is not necessary to prove apostolic succession. It is of more importance to identify our churches to-day with those of the first century than it is to trace the history through the centuries when there was no recorded history. The woman was driven into the wilderness for a season (Rev. 12:6). To illustrate: After the war General Lee lost a beautiful mare, whether strayed or stolen he did not know. He advertised for her, describing her color and size in detail. Deacon William Campbell, of Essex County, Virginia, read the advertisement and saw near his home an animal that exactly answered the description. He wrote General Lee, who sent his son from Lexington to investigate. As soon as he saw the animal he said, "That is father's mare." It was not at all necessary to follow the tracks of that mare from Lexington to Essex. The main thing was to identify her with the one that was lost. The Baptist churches of the New Testament were local, independent, self-governing, democratic organizations. The Baptists of to-day answer precisely to that description and they are the only such in Christendom.

Their *doctrines are scriptural*. Two symbolic ordinances did Jesus establish and enjoin—Baptism and the Lord's Supper. They are the most eloquent preachers God ever ordained. Baptism preaches a sermon under three divisions on the necessity for regeneration: (1) It speaks of the death, burial and resurrection of Christ; (2) it portrays the sinner's death and burial to sin and resurrection to walk in newness of life; (3) it prophesies that these bodies, after they are dead and buried shall rise again. It compasses the past, present and future. Nothing but immersion is adequate to this, and nothing but immersion is in the New Testament, the ablest Pedo-baptists themselves being witnesses. A minister preached a sermon in which he undertook to show that "in" and "into" did not mean immersion. He said, "John did not baptize Jesus in the Jordan, but close to, near by, round about Jordan. Philip and the Eunuch did not go down into the water, but close to, near by, round about." An Irishman in the congregation arose at the conclusion of the sermon and said, "Your Reverence, your sermon to-day has brought me much comfort. It explains many mysteries which have long perplexed me. I could never understand how Jonah could live in the whale for three days and nights. Now I see that he was not in the whale, but close to, near by, round about, swimming in the water. The Bible says the three Hebrew children were cast into the fiery furnace and I wondered how they lived. You have explained it. They were not actually in the furnace, but close to, near by, round about, where they could warm themselves. We read that Daniel was cast into the den of lions and why they did not devour him was a mystery to me. But he was not in the den at all, but only close to, near by, round about where he could hear them roar and feel no harm. Then, your Reverence, I am a very wicked man and have long been afraid of future punishment. You have relieved my apprehension. When the Bible says the wicked shall be cast into hell with all nations that forget God, I shall henceforth interpret it as meaning that I shall not actually go to hell, but only close to, near by, round about." That Irishman had the truth in his wit. It is perilous to explain away the Scripture.

The Lord's Supper, the other ordinance, is a sermon under three divisions upon the atoning death of Jesus: (1) It says that Jesus died for our sins according to the Scriptures; (2) it emphasizes our spiritual subsistence on him; (3) it expresses the hope that he will come again. Like baptism, the supper compasses the past, present and future. In its proper observance memory, faith and hope are operative. It is not a sacrament. It is emblematic of the atoning death of Jesus and preaches the doctrine of spiritual subsistence on him. When Jesus said, "This is my body," he no more meant his actual body than he meant a literal door when he said, "I am the door"; or a grape vine when he said, "I am the vine"; or a macadam road when he said, "I am the way." The Romanist doctrine of transubstantiation is untenable. How can an officiating priest change inert matter into both soul and deity when the Creator himself did not form man's soul from matter? If Christ died once for all, how can he die again every time the "mass" is celebrated? If Jesus ascended into heaven to remain there until the final restoration of all things, how can he be bodily present in the bread and wine? If Jesus meant what he said, *"All* ye drink of it," why does the priest withhold the cup from the people? Does not such practice violate the unity of the ordinance by excluding the wine from laymen though Christ used both emblems to set forth his doctrine? Are not the worship and adoration of mere

matter, bread and wine, as God, idolatry?
Dr. J. R. Graves and a Catholic priest were
debating the subject of the Lord's Supper.
The Catholic priest argued that when the
priest blessed the elements they became the
actual flesh and blood of the Lord. In his
rejoinder Dr. Graves held up a glass of wine
and said to the priest: "When you bless this
it becomes the blood of Christ. If the blood
of Christ it cannot be contaminated?" The
priest assented. Taking from his pocket a
bottle of poison, Dr. Graves poured its contents into the wine and said to the priest:
"You bless and drink half of this glass and I
will drink the other half." The priest did
not drink.

Historically, the order of the ordinances
was, first, Baptism, and then the Lord's
Supper. Logically, it should be so, because
birth, symbolized in baptism, comes before
nourishment, symbolized in the Lord's Supper. Neither ordinance has any saving
efficacy. They are for the saved, and by
their scriptural observance we keep alive and
promulgate vital truths of the gospel. We do
not bury a man to kill him; we bury him be-

cause he is dead. We do not bury him by sprinkling a little dirt on him; we put him under the ground. Had there been no perversion of the mode of baptism, there had been no question of restricted communion. Others must bear the responsibility for changing the meaning and mode and for the subsequent controversies.

Their *course has been consistent.* For the simple truth of the New Testament they have stood and suffered and died. In the Old World where the State controlled the church, as in England, or the church controlled the State, as in Rome, bonds, stripes, imprisonment and execution were their lot. In the New World it was little better until the acceptance of their principles made it so. The Episcopalians in Virginia and the Congregationalists in New England denied the freedom of conscience. The Baptists suffered severely. Patrick Henry rode from Hanover County to Fredericksburg, fifty miles, without renumeration to defend three imprisoned Baptist preachers. His better known speech in old St. John's had no more of dramatic power and convincing effect than his defense of these preachers. He entered the court room during the reading of the indictment by the prosecutor. After the prosecutor ended his brief, Henry took the paper and launched into a speech which moved the audience to sighs and tears and evoked from the judge the order, "Sheriff, discharge these men." Read two paragraphs of that speech:

"May it please Your Worship in a day like this, when Truth is about to burst her fetters; when mankind are about to be aroused to claim their natural and inalienable rights; when the yoke of oppression that has reached the wilderness of America and the unnatural alliance of ecclesiastical and civil power are about to be dissevered—at such a period when liberty, liberty of conscience, is about to wake from her slumberings and inquire into the reason of such charges as I find exhibited here to-day in this indictment—If I am not deceived—according to the contents of the paper I now hold in my hand—these men are accused of *preaching the gospel of the Son of God*. Great God!

"May it please Your Worship, there are periods in the history of man when corruption and depravity have so long debased the human character that man sinks under the weight of the oppressor's hand—becomes his servile, his abject slave. He licks the hand that smites him. He bows in passive obedience to the mandates of the despot; and, in this state of servility, he receives his fetters of perpetual bondage. But, may it please Your Worship, such a day has passed. From that period when our fathers left the land of their nativity for these American wilds— from the moment they placed their feet upon the American continent—from that moment despotism was crushed, the fetters of darkness were broken and heaven decreed that man should be free—free to worship God according to the Bible. In vain were all their sufferings and bloodshed to subjugate this New World if we, their offspring, must still be oppressed and persecuted. But, may it please Your Worship, permit me to inquire once more, For what are these men about to be tried? This paper says *for preaching the gospel of the Saviour to Adam's fallen race!*"

Joseph H. Crooker, Congregationalist, in his recent book, "Winning of Religious

Liberty," discussing the persecution of the Baptists in Connecticut, says: "It was in many respects far more reprehensible than the punishment of the Quakers. The Baptists were then as now an exceedingly earnest, orderly, God–fearing people. There were many points of contact between them and the Congregationalists. But there was radical difference respecting baptism. They rejected infant baptism, not as a mystical right, but as a seal and symbol of conversion and because they have a more generous view of God's providence and man's nature, children did not need to be christened to be saved from hell fire."

Governor Endicott, of Massachusetts, being asked by John Clarke what law of God or man he had broken, replied, "You have denied infant baptism and deserve death." Hezekiah Smith was "warned off from God's earth" by the sheriff of Haverhill, Mass. Two Baptist students were expelled from Yale College for attending the Baptist church at Canterbury, Conn., during vacation. Baptist students at the Naval Academy at Annapolis, Md., are inconvenienced and hampered in their desire to attend a Baptist church.   At present there is an unjust discrimination against all Protestant boys when they enter the academy. From June to October this plebe class are not permitted to attend any church service except at the naval chapel. The Catholic plebes are allowed to attend the Catholic church in the town. The worship at the naval chapel is Episcopalian in its form. The new superintendent has introduced the innovation this year, for the first time, of observing "Lent." This is very trying, especially to Baptists, who, as the illustrious Christian philosopher and renowned astronomer Sir Isaac Newton is said to have frequently remarked, "were the only Christians who had never symbolized with the Church of Rome." One marvels that the Secretary of the Navy does not right these wrongs.

Through all the periods of religious persecution, of the union of Church and State, growing out of the heresy of infant baptism, there sounded one clear, consistent, courageous, convincing voice crying: "Render unto Caesar the things that are Caesar's, and unto God the things that are God's. The church is a spiritual body, the State is a secular body; you cannot unite the two without irreparable injury to both. The soul is free. Man's supreme duty is to God. The State cannot lay its finger upon the conscience." By and by that voice was heard and heeded. "And they overcame him because of the blood of the Lamb, and because of the word of their testimony, and they loved not their life, even unto death." The first government in the world that allowed full liberty of conscience from principle to all men was established by Baptists in Rhode Island. James Madison, graduate of Princeton and preparing for the Episcopal ministry, was so shocked by the mistreatment of Baptists and so moved by their preaching through prison bars that he abandoned the ministry and became the political apostle of religious freedom in Virginia and America. The Baptists were the only denomination who supported him unwaveringly. Others helped in dis-establishment, but when it was proposed to assess taxes for all religious bodies, to use one of Billy Sunday's expressions, "They fell for it." Madison said the Presbyterian min-

isters were "as ready to keep up an establishment which is to take them in as they
were to pull down that which shut them
out." Baptists have never believed in, or
countenanced, the union of Church and State.
If all the people in Richmond were Baptists
but one, that one would be as free in religion
as the screaming sea gull of the sea. Aye,
and if I were the only person in Richmond
who held to believers' baptism, soul freedom,
and a church polity of the people, for the people, and by the people, I would stand like
Athanasius until a sufficient number con-
curred in those fundamentals to organize a
gospel church.

Their *mission has prospered*. God has
turned their misfortune into fortune. The
Kaiser looked upon the ruddy, stern faces of
countless American youths and inquired,
"What ship brought so many of those Americans over here?" "The Lusitania, Your
Majesty." Strange as it may sound, the
persecution of the Baptists gave religious
liberty to America. It drove Roger Williams
into the wilderness where he could found the
first free church in a free State in the history

of the world. It awakened Jefferson and
Madison and their co-laborers to the iniquities
of the union of Church and State, and brought
about dis-establishment. Dr. J. L. M. Curry
was seated next to the British statesman
John Bright at a dinner in London. Mr.
Bright inquired, "What distinct contribution
has America made to the science of government?" Dr. Curry thought a moment and,
mindful of other democracies that had sprung
up in Europe, replied, "The doctrine of religious liberty." Bright thought a moment
and remarked, "A tremendous contribution."
Yes, it was the greatest contribution of the
New World to the Old, of America to civilization, and it was pre-eminently a Baptist contribution. Bancroft correctly says: "Freedom of conscience, unlimited freedom of
mind, was from the first the trophy of the
Baptists."

The most popular book of 1918, written
by a Spaniard, contains this sentence, "The
philosophy of modern democracy is lay-
Christianity." That is a striking statement
of the Baptist position. We reject and oppose
sacerdotalism that puts a priest between a

soul and God, sacramentarianism that makes the ordinance vehicles of grace, and ecclesiasticism that puts a church between a sinner and salvation. We insist upon the right, ability and duty of each soul to approach God directly through the one mediator, Christ. We recognize no "orders" in the ministry and no such distinctions as "clergy" and "laity." All are brethren and equal in Christ. The application of the Baptist principle would abolish priestcraft and kingcraft.

The world was convulsed for four years in a struggle for the rights of the people. The man who was in the recent conflict from the first, who perceived the issues more clearly than any other, whose frankness alarmed the Turks, and whose fearlessness heartened the Christians, whose courage infuriated the Hohenzollerns, and whose determination unnerved the Hapsburgs, whose appeals kept the British workmen in the factories and placed Foch at the head of the allied armies, whose lips have voiced the most distinctly Christian sentiment of any peace envoy, whose heart beats in unison with the heart and whose hand joins with the hand of President Wilson in a pledge to punish the wrong-doers and bind the nations into a brotherhood that will cultivate peace and good will, instead of war and hate; that man is our Baptist brother, Lloyd-George. He said last year: "Tell the Baptists of America we are fighting for Baptist principles in this war." Are not these principles for which blood has been shed, and lives sacrificed, worth living for in America and in the world?

The attitude of Baptists towards unionizing the denominations is simple and clear. We are ready to unite tomorrow upon the New Testament as the sole authority of faith and practice. In 1699 the Baptists of Philadelphia replied to a letter from the Episcopalians invitatory to a union that two things "absolutely necessary in order thereunto" must be shown from Holy Scripture: "First, that the foundation of your church, with all the orders, officers, rites and ceremonies are of divine institution"; second, "that you give us clear and infallible proof from God's holy word that our Lord Jesus Christ hath given power and authority to any man, men, convocation or synod to make, constitute and set up any

other laws, orders, officers, rites and ceremonies in his church, besides those which he
hath appointed in his holy word; or to alter
or change those which he hath therein appointed." This Baptist reply remains un-
answered to this day. We will never unite
upon an extra and anti-scriptural program
framed in New York or elsewhere, as directors
would merge corporations. It is amusing
to see the unionists set up their Procustean
bed and begin lopping the large and stretch-
ing the small to make all uniform. An Episcopal bishop said in San Antonio some years
ago: "There ought to be but three denominations in the world: the Catholics, standing
on one side for the authority of the church;
the Baptists, standing on the other side for
the authority of the Bible; all the other denominations should be united, for the difference between them is the difference between
tweedledum and tweedledee." He was correct. There we take our stand and cannot
surrender or compromise our convictions; nor
would we have others do so. Jesus did not
pray for organic church union when he prayed
that prayer in the seventeenth chapter of

John that "all might be one." They were all baptized believers. They were one organically. They had uniformity without unity of spirit. Jesus prayed for unity of spirit, for freedom from rivalries, jealousies, animosities and antipathies. We pray the same prayer and seek to answer it by endeavoring to keep the unity of the spirit in the bonds of peace. Though we speak the truth, sometimes the unwelcome truth, we do so in love.

Their attitude towards governmental interference is now what it was in 1776, viz., religion is not within the purview of the civil power. The question is not, "Is religion necessary to the well-being of the State?" but, "Is religion advanced by government control or interference?" The third assistant secretary of war went beyond the proper bounds when he affirmed "the whole desire of the department is in the interest of breaking down, rather than emphasizing denominational distinction." It is none of the government's affair how many denominations there are so long as they obey the Constitution of the United States. The government's only concern with them is to see that they enjoy their guaranteed rights. The war department did an unconstitutional thing when it denied Baptists the right to minister to their young men in the camps. It did an unjust thing when it granted to the Catholics what it had denied to the Baptists. It did an unwise thing when it compelled and confined us to service through an organization that combined moving pictures, dancing, boxing, merchandise, social welfare, and religion, and which refused in some huts to allow a minister to call sinners to public profession of faith in Jesus Christ. The soldiers should know that while we gave our money freely, we had no voice or choice in the way it was expended. The government should know that the rights we waived in war times we still hold tenaciously and now proclaim fearlessly. The experience of history teaches that whenever the government has touched religion it has corrupted it. The logical end is the definition by the government of what the privileged may preach. This no Baptist can accept.

It behooves us to read again our history,

to baptize our minds afresh in our immortal
principles, and to contend earnestly, though
lovingly, for the "faith which was once for
all delivered unto the saints." "With malice
towards none and charity towards all; with
faith in the right as God gives us to see the
right"; asking nothing for ourselves that we
do not concede to all others; regarding every
soul as a human brother and every saved soul
as a Christian brother; with loyalty to the
truth as it is incorporated in the New Testament and with allegiance to Jesus Christ, our
only Lord,

> "We lift our banner to the air,
> And swear to guard our legacy."

VIII.

THE CHALLENGE OF THE CHANGING ORDER.

"Unto whomsoever much is given, of him shall much be required." The principles of Baptists commit them to a large program. The whole gospel for the whole world is that program. No people profess more by their doctrines. We are under obligations to match profession with practice. The world, Christian and non-Christian, has a right to demand works as proof of our faith. Unless we can show results we must give place to those who can. This is not merely a cold, commercial rule; it was the acid test of Jesus: "By their fruits ye shall know them." The truth is not to be wrapped in a napkin for safe-keeping; in such manner will it be lost. The truth is to be promulgated. The Providence church suffered for energetic leadership and vigorous evangelism and lost its existence. The Newport church was blessed with aggressive leadership and evangelistic passion and remains a fount of healing.

Jordan marked the beginning of Christ's ministry. The three busiest, most useful years ever lived on earth followed his baptism by John. They were years crowded with praying, teaching, preaching, healing, saving. He trained the disciples in the lessons of the kingdom and then commanded them to go work everywhere under the power he would send upon them. They stayed until persecution thrust them forth. Then they went everywhere preaching the word. Multitudes were saved; churches sprang up like magic, old systems of error crumbled, and the empire was converted from the worship of Caesar to the worship of Christ.

Jesus' command to go "make disciples" is as binding as his command to "baptize"; and it comes first. When all Baptists are as insistent on the "go" as some are on the "baptize" they will conquer the world for Christ. That is to say, their mission will be fulfilled when orthopraxy equals orthodoxy. This is not to decry orthodoxy. It is folly to proclaim unless one has a vital doctrine to announce; but woe to him who has such a doctrine and neglects its proclamation! He may hear Jesus say: "Cast ye the unprofitable servant into outer darkness; there shall be weeping and gnashing of teeth."

A Baptist who is not missionary to the heart of his being and to the tips of his fingers denies the faith and is no Baptist at all. Nor is he Christian. Anti-missionary Christian is a misnomer. Anti-missionary is anti-Christ; for the only Christ we know is the Christ of the gospels and he embraced the "world" in his plan of salvation. You mutilate the gospel when you confine it to one nation, race or hemisphere, or to the "elect" of the earth. Calvinism is a comforting, strengthening doctrine, but ultra-Calvinism is a blight. Our duty is to invite all to salvation and leave God to do the drawing. Spurgeon was right: "The question for me is not, are the heathen lost without the gospel, but am I saved if I have the gospel and fail to give it to them." The old negro had a very practical and scriptural doctrine. Asked if he believed in election, he answered: "Yes, but I hab noteeced ain't no man been 'lected ter office whut wan't er candedate."

Stinginess is the root of much "omission-aryism." Such people love money more than they love lost souls. God created the world out of nothing; He made order out of chaos; He formed man out of the dust of the ground; He caused water to gush forth from the rock; He performed every kind of miracle; but even God, with all His power, cannot use a stingy man or woman. Covetousness dries up the fountains of spirituality and parches the life with barrenness; it shrivels the soul; it mars the countenance; it paralyzes religious energy; it makes men idolaters; it bars the gates of heaven; it smoothes the way and opens the portals to hell. Bad everywhere, it is worse when it attaches to the minister. He becomes a "watch dog" for his church. He pleads their poverty, the pressure of local demands, the multiplicity of outside calls, the untimeliness of the present object. He becomes captious about methods, expenses, waste, management, persons. All the time he is holding up a mirror in which every one but himself sees himself. "Not greedy of

filthy lucre," was one of Paul's qualifications
of a pastor.

American Baptists are being weighed in the
balances of material prosperity. Our people
share in the unprecedented prosperity of the
country. They possess conveniences and com-
forts, and many of them enjoy luxuries.
Very well, so long as their spiritual growth
keeps pace with their material growth. John
had a standard for a Christian's wealth:
"Beloved, I pray above all things that thou
mayest prosper and be in health, even as thy
soul prospereth." He prayed for the good
health and financial success of Gaius, but
only "as" his soul prospered. The thought
is similar to that in the prayer "forgive us
our debts *as* we forgive our debtors." The
measure of the divine forgiveness is com-
mensurate with the human forgiveness. So
the degree of temporal prosperity is to be
proportionate to that of spiritual prosperity.
Sam Jones said, "No man worth more than
$50,000 can be saved." That is purely
arbitrary. A man may have as much property as he acquires honestly and uses right-
eously. Baptists successfully triumphed over

State and Church persecution. What shall
be the issue of the conflict with prosperity?
Only as they "seek first the kingdom of God,"
only as they administer their wealth as trus-
tees of their Lord, only as they grow in
liberality as they increase in worldly goods
will they emerge victorious. The law of
giving is as obligatory upon the boy making
fifty dollars a month as it is upon the man
making fifty hundred. It is a larger law than
tithing and should yield more than the mere
tithe. Every one, young and old, rich and
poor, male and female, is to give systematical-
ly and weekly as "the Lord has prospered."
When we are as scriptural in giving as we are
in baptizing we will be the most efficient
denomination in Christendom. Pastors will
be freed from temporal things to give themselves to prayer and the ministry of the word.
They will preach with greater power when a
generous support relieves them of financial
embarrassment. The ranks of the ministry
will be recruited, not indeed by hirelings,
but by young men called of God to preach
and encouraged by a denomination that does
not "muzzle the ox that treadeth out the

corn." The stakes will be strengthened in the home land and the cords lengthened in foreign lands. Mission and Educational Boards will have funds ample for their needs and the kingdom of God will be established in the earth. My soul exults in the thought! A mighty host of New Testament Christians impassioned with zeal for Christ and love for the lost, holding all they have as under tribute to their King, counting not their lives dear unto themselves, finishing their ministry with joy and blessing!

The alternative causes my soul to shudder. A people strong in doctrine and numbers but flabby in deeds and efficiency. A tree, large of trunk and beautiful of foliage, but a cumberer of the ground. A light to shine to the remotest corners of the earth, but "light become darkness." A well of water to spring up to eternal life but the waters are dried up and the thirst unquenched. A sea for boats and fishes, for joy and trade, but with no outlet until its waters are dead and its shores are salt.

"I looked upon a sea, and lo! it was dead,
  Although by Hermon's snows and Jordan fed!
  How came a fate so dire?   The tale's soon told;
  All it got it kept, and fast did hold.

"All tributary streams found here their grave,
  For this sea received, but nothing gave.
  Oh! sea that's dead, teach me to know and feel
  That selfish grasp and greed my doom will seal."

The war demonstrated America's ability
to mobilize quickly vast resources of men and
materials.   The churches were active in that
mobilization.   The fact is, the government
called and relied greatly upon the churches to
counteract enemy propaganda, to awaken
patriotism, to facilitate enlistment, to aid
food conservation, to subscribe to government
bonds and war savings stamps, and to contribute to Red Cross, War Work Council,
and Syrian and Armenian Relief. Baptist
churches, as others, rallied to the call.   They
never wearied or counted the cost.   It is to
their everlasting credit.   They must now key
themselves to the spiritual notes of the kingdom as they did to the martial notes of
democracy.   They must combine and direct
on missions and Christian education the

tremendous energies they readily directed
upon war. The task of the Baptists is to
bring their thoughts, made capacious by
world problems, into captivity to Christ; to
harness loosened powers to kingdom enterprises. May it not be that providential events
are preparing us for the program of Jesus,
"into all the world," "unto all the nations."

President Wilson has become the world
spokesman for political democracy. In out-
lining to Congress the aims before America
in the war, he mentioned three principles
that are particularly dear to Baptists: (1)
the rights of the small nations; (2) the right
of every people to determine their own form
of government and to choose their rulers; (3)
the safety of the world for democracy. These
are cherished and immemorial Baptist principles. (1) Among us the smallest church
has equal rights with the largest church;
the youngest church member has equal rights
with the oldest; (2) every church governs its
own affairs and determines its co-operation;
every individual not only has the privilege,
but is under the imperious duty of determining for himself his religion and choosing his

church; (3) our whole history expounds the doctrines of democracy—the rule of a majority of the people; and we have striven to create conditions in which that doctrine could live and flourish.

A practical question for the nations and Baptists is, "What type of democracy is safe for the world?" Drunk with the new wine of freedom, long suppressed peoples of Europe are destroying every right of property and violating every form of law. So quickly have they come into power that they squander it like prodigal heirs suddenly possessed of a large estate. Democracy to unenlightened, lawless people is like a razor in the hands of a child. Baptists have two advantages in the changing order: (1) their type of democracy is that of Jesus and Paul; (2) they are experienced in its administration. The first time in history the word "democracy" occurs in a civil document is when John Clarke wrote it in the preamble and act of incorporation of the Providence Plantations: "The form of government established in Providence Plantations is *democratic*; that is to say, a government held by the free and voluntary consent of all or the greater part of the free inhabitants"; * * * "the government which this body politic doth attend unto in this Island * * * is a *democracy*, or popular government." That was the first opportunity of Baptists to form a government on their plan. The administration of that democracy was in the interest of public order. A distinction between civil and religious offenses was carefully guarded. Citizenship was refused the anarchist Gorton. Religious freedom does not mean fanaticism; civil freedom does not mean anarchy. Baptists can never be Bolshevists, nor countenance any such. Baptists hold that freedom of action is delimited by the rights of others and license is regulated by law; property is sacred and the person is inviolable.

Baptists must promote education so that intelligence will be the handmaid of experience. Baptists are the last of all the denominations to depreciate learning. Where one man, or group of men, governs, their wisdom may guide affairs aright. Where the people govern it is essential that the masses shall be enlightened in order to rule wisely and well.

Primary education, State education, Denominational education find in us firm friends. We only insist that what is taught shall be knowledge, not speculation; constructive, not destructive; that denominational schools shall be Christian in fact, not in name alone. To make sure of the future we must put a premium upon Christian education. A denomination without its system of schools and colleges and theological seminaries is a denomination without a future. Baptists should never forget that the founder of those little Christian democracies that dotted the shores of the Mediterranean was the best educated man of his time; and that a Greek Testament in the hand of a college graduate was the immediate cause of the organization of the Baptist denomination in America.

Times change, but principles are eternal and admit of application to all conditions. We must so teach and exemplify our doctrines as to make them attractive and powerful. Autonomous church government relates itself to other like bodies and forms a co-operating group. The spiritual significance of the ordinances constitutes their highest value; spirituality in individuals and churches vitalizes the ordinances. On one side of the shield is "Preservation of the Saints"; on the other is "Let every one that hath this hope in him purify himself even as he is pure." Salvation by grace imposes a debt of gratitude upon the beneficiary which is discharged only by its zealous proclamation. Sanctification is a process in which believers grow in grace unto perfection attained when they "awake in his likeness." In the doing of these things we both save ourselves and them that hear us. The love that seeks and finds flows from the redeemed in streams of sympathy and service.

The upheaval over the earth obliterated much hoary injustice but left conditions unsettled, even chaotic. These present a challenging opportunity. For Baptists to waver now would be criminal; for them to surrender would be suicidal. We may profit by the example of the American forces in the great Niagara of war. The general temper of that army was sacrificial and heroic. From the hour General Pershing offered to Genera Foch all that America had in France, and the larger numbers who were coming, from that hour the clouds began to lift. The day we lay our all upon the altar of Christ to be used as he directs will be the day when the kingdom will come with power.

We may learn also from the method of training the American army. Some attention was given to defense, but much more to offense. Therein is the real secret of the Americans' signal success. They went to Europe to drive the Germans out of France and Belgium. General Bundy sounded the note that won the war. On being ordered by a superior officer at Chateau-Thierry to retreat, he replied: "Retreat! We have just come. We came not to retreat, but to advance."

"Is this the time, O Church of Christ, to sound
   Retreat? To arm with weapons cheap and blunt
   The men and women who have borne the brunt
Of Truth's fierce strife, and nobly held their ground?
Is this the time to halt, when all around
   Horizon's lift, new destinies confront,
   Stern duties wait our nation, never wont
To play the laggard, when God's will was found?

"No! rather strengthen stakes and lengthen cords.
  Enlarge thy plans and gifts, O thou elect,
    And to thy kingdom come for such a time!
The earth with all its fullness is the Lord's.
  Great things attempt for Him, great things expect,
  Whose love imperial is, Whose power sublime."